JULIÁ

IS THERE HOPE?

The Fascination
of the Discovery

HAB

ISBN 978-1-941457-22-1

Translation by: Sheila Beatty

INTRODUCTION

"Death and life have contended in that combat stupendous."[1] With these words the Christian Easter liturgy concisely describes the exceptional nature of the event it celebrates. Its exceptional nature is highlighted by the fact that there was never any *real* combat between death and life. It is just a poetic expression, because we know from the outset who the winner is. Can it be a true contest when we know the result in advance?

You need not wait until the last day to realize it. Young people become aware of it quite early. I observed this recently when I met a group of high school seniors online. They already perceive the first symptoms of the void that looms over their days, like a foretaste of death. "My life is slowing losing its color." "The initial enthusiasm has been waning for some time now; I don't have the drive I used to have." "I'm totally apathetic. Nothing touches me or attracts me." And yet they are not resigned. Paradoxically, the acute perception of the symptoms sparks their desire for life. They have it in the DNA of their humanity, as we do, and it explodes like a question they cannot hold back. "What can truly destroy the boredom and apathy, and make me begin living again?" They may be young, but they are already the explicit battleground between the yearning for life and the fear that everything ends in

[1] The Mass of Easter Day, "Victimae paschali laudes" sequence. https://bible.usccb.org/bible/readings/040118.cfm

nothingness. Unlike them, we adults have enough history behind us to know that any attempt of ours will be too weak. The end is a given: death always emerges victorious. This is why I said the word combat is really a euphemism here.

In this context, you can grasp the meaning and audacity of the Easter liturgy. "It is a fact that if Christ had not risen, the 'emptiness' would be set to prevail. If we take away Christ and His resurrection, there is no escape for man, and every one of his hopes remains an illusion. Yet today is the day [the day of Easter] when the proclamation of the Lord's resurrection vigorously bursts forth, and it is the answer to the recurring question of the sceptics, that we also find in the book of Ecclesiastes, 'Is there a thing of which it is said, *See, this is new?*' (Ec 1:10). We answer, yes, on Easter morning, everything was renewed. 'Death and life have come face to face in a tremendous duel: the Lord of life was dead, but now He lives triumphant' (Easter Sequence). This is what is new! A newness that changes the lives of those who accept it."[2]

Without the resurrection of Christ there would be no real combat. Let's be clear: the announcement of the "fact" does not predetermine the combat that takes place in each of us. Rather, it makes the combat possible and unleashes it.

So now, we have to ask ourselves whether the announcement of the resurrection of Christ is still credible for people today, who claim the full use of their reason and freedom. The answer requires that we look to history, to our personal experience, because

---

[2] Benedict XVI, *Urbi et Orbi Message, Easter 2009,* April 12, 2009.

only here will we see the reasons the announcement trustworthy or not. In life, in concrete experience, the announcement must demonstrate its credibility.

Paradoxically, the pandemic has offered us a propitious opportunity for this verification. In fact, we are witnessing a full blown clash between being and nothingness: a unique combat because of its import and dimensions, with a more visible part constantly covered by the mass media–the death statistics, the maxed out intensive care units, the difficulties of the economy–and a more hidden and personal part with its aspects of fear, solitude, fragility and the connected gush of questions that have shaken certainties that seemed rock solid. We can summarize them in one question, which is the most widespread and challenging in this time dominated by uncertainty: *is there hope*?

The question became the theme of the Spiritual Exercises of the university students of the Movement, and later that of the adults of the Fraternity of Communion and Liberation. Many people felt deeply challenged by it and contributed with letters and testimonies, as you can see reading the text.

The impact with the harshness of the reality made our human need emerge with greater clarity. In one way or another, we are all dealing with the question about hope. There is nothing more crucial for our life. If we do not succeed in finding an adequate answer, death will never cease hanging over our heads like the sword of Damocles, hanging over every human experience of ours, no matter how true, above all the most significant experiences.

Thus, out of passion for life, out of the desire not to be resigned to spending every moment crushed by the fear of death, by the void of meaning, we decided to look this question in the face, as women and men who have no intention of losing their lives living, and who expect no shortcuts. Years ago Fr. Giussani said, "When we get together, why do we do so? So as to tear out from our friends, and if it were possible from the whole world, the nothingness in which all men find themselves."[3] This is the impetus that supports the itinerary in the following pages, conceived as a way to help us not sell ourselves short, not give up on the desire for life, remaining open to the fascination of the discovery of a credible answer to our expectant awaiting in which our nature as human beings is expressed.

[3] L. Giussani, *"Why Do We Gather Together? To Free Ourselves from Evil. The One Who Freed Us Is Christ"* [Message for the Macerata-Loreto pilgrimage], June 14, 2003, *Traces*, n. 7/2003.

CHAPTER 1

"EVEN WORSE THAN THIS CRISIS IS THE TRAGEDY OF SQUANDERING IT"

"Even worse than this crisis is the tragedy of squandering it by closing in on ourselves."[1] These words of Pope Francis impel us to become more conscious of what has happened to us, of what we have experienced in this last year or so.

1. The impact with reality

From the very beginning, we have faced this challenge, which has allowed no one to remain indifferent, with a working hypothesis expressed in a line by Fr. Giussani:[2] "If an individual were to barely live the impact with reality, because, for example, he had not had to struggle, he would scarcely possess a sense of his own consciousness, would be less aware of his reason's energy and vibration." Thus, following Giussani, we are invited to "live always the real intensely,"[3] without negating or precluding anything. In fact, it is one

[1] Francis, *Pentecost Homily*, May 31, 2020.
[2] Cf. J. Carrón, *Reawakening Our Humanity. Reflections in a Dizzying Time*, trans. Kristin Hurd (Milan: Fraternità di Comunione e Liberazione, 2020).
[3] L. Giussani, *The Religious Sense*, trans. John Zucchi (Montreal: McGill-Queen's University Press, 1997), 100, 108.

thing to be unable to ignore or avoid the impact with the circumstance, but it is entirely another thing to live it, embracing the provocation it bears.

With this hypothesis to verify, even such a dangerous situation as that generated by Covid paradoxically could become an opportunity to increase our self-awareness, so often obscured, and to perceive more powerfully the energy and vibration of our reason; in other words, it could become an opportunity for the reawakening of the human, as consciousness, reason and affection.

What has happened? After more than a year, what have we seen happen in and around us?

Many people have noted two phases, two faces of our experience in front of the pandemic, corresponding to the two waves of the spread of the virus. The second wave, as Antonio Scurati observed, "caught us not less unprepared and not less immature than the first wave, but more tired, demoralized, quarrelsome, and petty,"[4] as if we had failed to learn from what happened in the first phase and grow, failed to increase our awareness and become more substantial ourselves. This can be sensed from what emerged during the second wave: a greater sense of fragility, the spread of uncertainty and anxiety, signs that indicate, as noted by Massimo Recalcati, that "the true trauma is not in the past but in the future." The second wave, "destroying the illusion of the renewal of life that we all had believed in, [...] extended the horizon of the nightmare. The second time of the trauma is more traumatic than the

---

[4] A. Scurati, "Un Natale severo (e di speranza) [A Harsh (and Hopeful) Christmas]," *Corriere della Sera*, November 20, 2020, p. 11.

first because it shows that the evil was not spent, but is still alive among us. The hopes nourished by the summer have been dashed. Today this disappointment is the prevalent sentiment."[5]

For a certain time we were used to living in a state of apparent safety, with the illusion of being able to dominate reality. As the virus broke onto the scene, it gave this illusion a big shove. However, after the first wave, it did not take much to convince us that we had the situation in hand again, and thus that a return to normal life was imminent. So we enjoyed the summer, some more, others less, but "One does not know what one knows, or even what one wishes to know, until one is challenged."[6]

The second wave once again crushed the dream or presumption, reminding us definitively that we do not control reality. As Cesare Cornaggia observed, "It was thought that death was a matter of chance, like a tumor or an accident, and that infectious diseases had been defeated; instead, the unknown that we do not see, and to which we do not know how to respond, kills us. This is the source of our insecurity."[7]

Thus "insecurity about the future" grew in proportion to the "sense of the unknown." At the beginning of the second wave, Edgar Morin also photographed

[5] M. Recalcati, "Il trauma della seconda ondata. Se cresce la paura del futuro [The Trauma of the Second Wave. Growing Fear for the Future]," *la Repubblica*, October 31, 2020, p. 28.

[6] Th. Wilder, *The Woman of Andros. The Ides of March* (London: Capucin Classics, 2006), digital edition.

[7] C.M. Cornaggia, "Ansia, paura, insicurezza: ecco quel che ancora non sappiamo [Anxiety, Fear, Insecurity: What we still don't know]," interview by Paolo Vites, *ilsussidiario.net*, November 8, 2020.

the end of the illusion with the word "insecurity." He wrote, "We have entered an era of great insecurity," underlining "the multidimensional character of the crisis that touches the life of every single individual, of all nations and of the entire planet […]. We are all part of this adventure, full of ignorance, the unknown, lunacy, reason, mystery, dreams, joy, and pain. And insecurity."[8] Notwithstanding the reassurance of certain discourses, the optimism that accompanied the discoveries of science and the initiatives of the pharmaceutical industry, anguish still lurks in our hearts, threatening.

After more than a year, we are still navigating by sight, not knowing how long this pandemic will last, though fortunately there are increasingly concrete signs of a way out. We will have to wait and see, and like everyone else hope things get better as soon as possible. However, the situation I have described, which has involved the life of people, society and the entire world so extensively, has brought forth from the inner workings of our lived experience a question that accompanies the existence of the human person: is there hope?

The title of our Spiritual Exercises, "Is there hope?" resonated in us and others who were invited to participate, as happened in December on the occasion of the Spiritual Exercises for University Students. A classmate told a person who invited her, "You people always focus on a point that touches something inside me. This theme is crucial!" Another person said, "The

8 E. Morin, "Il potere dell'incertezza [Power and Uncertainty]", *la Repubblica*, October 1, 2020, p. 27.

title proposed reverberated in me; it is the question that has accompanied this time."

This question resonates from the depths of our daily struggles. A friend wrote me, "Beginning last October, with the situation of the pandemic starting to worsen once again and the spreading general violence that increasingly characterized the news, this question burned in me: 'Do I hope that things have a good destiny?' Unfortunately, I found myself answering, 'I don't know.' Many people have died and still today, after a year, continue to die of Covid. Many friends, of myself and my husband, people dear to us, have been gravely impacted by the economic crisis. In addition, some very painful news and big difficulties I've been going through, in particular at work, have led me to say, 'I'm not sure any more that things have a good destiny; everything is telling me the opposite.' I understand that deep down this question reveals my fear that things, relationships and those dearest to me end up in nothingness. In the beginning I resisted admitting to myself that I had this question. Honestly, I was very ashamed of it. Then I remembered that in my life the most important steps began with uncomfortable, unusual and very serious questions. What most 'encouraged' me to look at my question was you: in fact, when I discovered you had chosen 'Is there hope?' as the title of the Spiritual Exercises, I thought, 'Here's a man who not only is unafraid to ask himself this question, but he's also unafraid to ask it of everyone.' I felt that you were at once a father, because you helped me not fear looking at myself and loving the questions I have. As the months have passed, this question has burned more and more, and I'm sorry to admit I still don't know how to answer it. So, I'd like to ask you what can help me grasp it."

I'll tell you right away that the first help comes from the question itself, as many of you have written me. "The question about hope strikes me because of its power. Once again, the question frees us from our partial gaze, to open us to something else. It's up to us to choose to follow its impact or to muffle it. The question seems more pertinent than ever, and I don't want to miss this opportunity." Another person stressed, "I realize that the work on the question you proposed has already begun marking my days, making me more attentive and open to what happens." Another person observed, "The problem is to let the question impose itself, let it establish itself where it believes it best, without giving us any relief. 'Is there hope?' It is a battle to allow this question to enter. It is a battle not to push it out of my days. It is a battle not to lie and therefore tell myself that deep down there is no hope, and then pretend that there is, because it's easier that way."

2. Attitudes in front of what has happened

Each of us is called to respond personally to the question "Is there hope?" observing ourselves in action, taking note of the way we look at and face life, which gives nobody a free ticket. So then, first of all let's review the attitudes that have emerged in ourselves or in others in response to what has happened, and that have to some degree also been ours. This will help us have a clearer awareness of the question, its pertinence to life, and the road we need to follow in order to respond to it.

a) The temptation to remove the datum

The cover of the December 14 issue of the famous US magazine, *Time*, featured "2020" written in black in big block numbers and crossed out with a red X, and under it in smaller letters the subtitle, "The Worst Year Ever." A symbolic X was placed over the past year as if to express the desire to eliminate it. But as everyone knows, there is no way to erase three million deaths and the economic crisis provoked by the pandemic, the worst effects of which we may not have experienced yet! "This is the story of a year you'll never want to revisit," Stephanie Zacharek wrote in the first line of her editorial.[9]

There is always the temptation to erase the things that force us to ask ourselves what gives meaning to life. A university student wrote, "For the last twenty-one days since isolation began because of Covid, every night before going to bed I've asked myself whether there's hope in my life. These have been difficult days. The illness has been pretty severe with me. For this reason, my initial answer was clearly, 'No, there is no hope.' This period was just a moment to be erased. I lived it in survivor mode, waking up, feeding myself, bathing and working, then going back to bed and repeat it all the next day. Tomorrow I'll be free, but–and it's a big but–I wonder whether twenty-one

[9] S. Zacharek, "2020. The Worst Year Ever," *Time*, December 14, 2020.

days lived in a certain way have nullified my being what I am." The experience of many was marked by a tendency to survive and, once the worst was over, to remove the moment lived, with a consequent weakening of the perception of self and suspicion about one's future.

Others did not want to close their eyes and did not try to forget, but on the contrary, wanted the circumstance not to have happened in vain. "I'll tell you right off that this year has been an opportunity for me to realize as never before how fragile and limited I am, but I can't say this sentiment's been bad for me. On the contrary, it's made me discover how much I needed, and need, to found my life on something other than myself, on a fullness I don't build myself, that does not depend on the circumstances, that does not depend on me, and that bears up!"

b) Sadness and fear

In this period many feelings have come to the surface with insistence and have been difficult to contain. Perhaps we have never truly admitted to ourselves that we feel them, or have done little to explore them, comforted by the favorable changes underway. The Spanish journalist Salvador Sostres wrote, "For the first time, I spoke with a friend about the disappointment and sadness, and for the first time we don't know what to say or do. We're very tired because we haven't slept much, and we realize that up until today, we had never absolutely doubted our ability to do something with our own strength."[10]

An unease has risen to the surface, one that actually was already there inside us, covered by a veil, protected by a form of life, by a social rhythm that suddenly disappeared, thus allowing it to emerge. It has spread in many people, setting down roots, with a dark sense of oneself and one's destiny, almost a perception of nothingness, like the projection of an oppressive shadow on the future, as described well in the words of Karmelo C. Iribarren. "Now I think as I look / through the open window / at the highway, watching / how the cars flash their headlights / in the last section / before the tunnel. I think / that this is life, / and that there's nothing else. A weak / light blink of light toward the shadow / at greater or lesser velocity."[11] Therefore, is life nothing more than a journey toward darkness? Is it only the speed that changes?

The fear for oneself and one's future, linked to the perception of the threat and the forced discovery of one's vulnerability, has in many cases also seeped into many homes, affecting the closest relationships, as the writer and dramatist Francesco Piccolo confessed. "Before the pandemic, if anyone was afraid, it was maybe my children, fearful of me. […] Now […] I

---

[10] S. Sostres, "La próxima vez que me muera," *ABC*, September 24, 2020. Our translation from the Italian translation.

[11] "Lo pienso ahora que miro / por la ventana abierta / la autopista, viendo / cómo los coches parpadean / en el último tramo, / antes de túnel. Pienso / que así es la vida, / y que no hay más. Un leve / guiño de luz hacia la sombra / a mayor o menor velocidad." K.C. Iribarren, "Hacia la sombra," in Id., *Seguro que esta historia te suena* (Salamanca: Renacimiento, 2015), 42. Our translation from the Italian translation.

instinctively keep my distance from them. Sometimes my son invites a classmate home to study, and I almost always try to return home after his friend has left. […] My daughter is in Bologna. […] She never calls me because she's so struck by my fear that she's afraid I think if she phones me I'll get infected. […] At times, I think I'm part of a TV series. […] I am not at all reassured by having a son at home who runs around, yells and goes out every day. This is the new contorted and unnatural tangle of sentiments that the coronavirus has created: being afraid of your own children more than of any other human being in the world."[12]

c) The terror of death

What fear are we talking about? Not only that of being infected, but that of dying, given that the consequences of infection can be lethal. Death, which we had carefully hidden and cast out, is once again visible. Massively present in real life and the media, it is no longer considered in the collective subconscious as a mere blip along the way, a sporadic inconvenience that still happens but soon will be eradicated or at least limited. To mark this, the Italian magazine *L'Espresso* chose "Life and Death" as "person of the year, 2020." The cover showed a "photograph" of hooded Death playing chess with a baby under an oppressive gray sky. Under it, the words "Fear of the end has overturned

---

[12] F. Piccolo, "Maledetto virus mi hai insegnato ad avere paura dei miei figli [This cursed virus that taught me to fear my own children], *la Repubblica*, February 1, 2021, pp. 12-13.

economic and political systems, and our daily existence." In the editorial, we read that death, "removed
by culture, [...] "has been brought "back to the center"
by "the year of the pandemic." Further on, we read
that the fear of the end, paradoxically, should bring
with it also a strange presentiment. "Being afraid of
death means knowing there is something that transcends our individual existence. An End. And the
Heirs."[13] In his article, Massimo Cacciari points out,
"Leopardi was the one who taught us. [...] If life truly
is worth something, that is, if it is intent on reaching
something that always transcends finite existence,
then one does not fear death, *one lives it*."[14] And living
it, the deep questions are reawakened.

d) *The reawakening of the deep questions*

Heschel observed, "The first answer to the question
'Who is man?' is the following: man is a being who
asks questions about himself. In asking such questions,
man discovers he is a person, and their quality reveals
his condition to him."[15] The human being is that level
of nature in which nature asks questions about itself,
its own meaning, its own origin and its own destiny.
"Why am I here? What is at stake in my existence? This
question does not derive from any premise: it is given

[13] "Persone dell'anno. La morte e la vita [People of the Year: Death and Life]",
cover title of *L'Espresso*, December 20, 2020.
[14] M. Cacciari, "Per amore della Vita [For the Love of Life]," *L'Espresso*, December 20, 2020, p. 17.
[15] A.J. Heschel, *Chi è l'uomo?* [Who is man?] (Milano: SE, 2005), 42. Our
translation from the Italian.

together with existence."[16] But the question about the meaning of one's own life cannot be separated from the one about the meaning of one's own death.

Those who have let themselves be struck by the immensity of the provocation of this dramatic year have not been able to avoid seeing questions arise in themselves, in their own consciousness, that in times defined as "normal" they might have spared themselves. But this time, with the global character of the danger, our flesh or that of someone close to us has been touched more directly and insistently by vulnerability, solitude, suffering and death. The situation has reawakened everyone from the daily torpor that often reduces the density of the existential questions and makes them seem like the exaggeration of those who want to ruin the party of living for everybody else. This bubble has popped, above all with the crash of the second wave. "Suffering is an aggression that invites us to awareness,"[17] Claudel reminds us.

Ignacio Carbajosa served as a priest for five weeks in a Covid-19 hospital in Madrid, and wrote in his diary about his experience as a "privileged witness" of the life and death of many people. He wrote, "What I saw fought within me. It wounded me." What did he see? Among many things, he saw a day-old baby girl and not an hour later he saw a woman who had just died, Elena. He asked himself, "Elena? Where are you, Elena? The two extremes of life, birth and death in less

---

[16] *Ibid*, p. 25. Our translation from the Italian.

[17] P. Claudel, *Tre figure sante per il tempo moderno* [Three holy figures for the modern age] (Alba (Cn): Paoline, 1997), 46. Our translation of the Italian translation.

than an hour. What a temptation to eliminate one of the two poles! And what courage and a challenge for reason, to keep both and open yourself to the question of 'What is man, that you think of him?'." After a month spent assisting Covid-19 patients, he noted in his diary, "In this period, my reason and affection have been challenged by a problem of knowledge: What is pain? What is death? And consequently, what is life? Every day I have to look this question in the face, staying in front of sick people who suffer and die."[18]

In these times, those who have not closed in on themselves like a hedgehog will have felt deep down inside the vibration of chords they did not know they had. Maybe some will have immediately silenced them in the attempt to return to normalcy. But they felt the reverberation nonetheless, even if for only a moment, like a miniscule seed, almost a nothing, the beginning of a reawakening of the human, as I observed before. "Precisely because of the difficulties I was not spared, for me 2020 coincided with an unexpected reawakening of my 'I'." Who knows how many people recognized it, and who knows how much time it will take for that seed to germinate?

I understand that this may seem too little in front of the vastness of the drama, but it is like a promise. In fact, the vibration of our innermost being is the sign of an expectant awaiting that is deeply rooted in us, one that coincides with ourselves: the expectant awaiting for something commensurate with life and death, the expectancy for something unforeseen that unleashes

---

[18] I. Carbajosa, *Testimone privilegiato* [Privileged Witness] (Castel Bolognese (Ra): Itaca, 2020), 16, 66, 96. Our translation.

a gush of affection for ourselves and enables our desire to reawaken and fulfill itself. This vibration of our reason, the urgent need for meaning that we have perceived with evidence in some moment, places us in a more favorable condition for glimpsing the answer, if and where it happens. In this context, Giussani often repeated a line by Reinhold Niebuhr. "Nothing is more unbelievable than the answer to a question that is not asked."[19] What does this mean? Today maybe we can understand it better, precisely because of the experience of the last year: the more I perceive a problem, the more a need throbs within me, the more I am attentive to any echo of a response. Any hint of an answer evokes my curiosity.[20]

It should not be forgotten that even with all its urgency and even though it is inevitable, the question about the meaning of existence contains an invitation that can be refused. And refusal leads to the thinning of the consciousness of that question, to the point of its disappearance. "The question imposes itself, but not attention to the question. Thus more than one person defines it as lazy [...]. So then the query about the meaning of existence thins out and finally vanishes. As Gide said, one reaches the point of "no-longer-feeling-

---

[19] R. Niebuhr, *The Nature and Destiny of Man. A Christian Interpretation*, vol. II (London-New York: Library of Theological Ethics, 1943), 6.

[20] Luigi Maria Epicoco observes, "The objective of the moment is not to survive contagion, but rather to understand that, also through this experience, we can no longer postpone the great question of the meaning of life that this pandemic is energetically bringing back to attention." (L.M. Epicoco in conversation with S. Gaeta, *La speranza non è morta. Parole di fede in tempo di crisi* [Hope is not dead. Words of faith in a time of crisis] (Cinisello Balsamo (Mi): San Paolo, 2020), 40. Our translation.

the-need."[21] Those who do not run from the question instead experience the cognitive heft, the capacity for waking up again. "In this 'heretofore unknown' year, a revolution has happened for me. I no longer need to close down a line of thought quickly, offering myself answers that are perfect and impeccable, but pre-packaged. Rather, I need exactly the opposite, to keep the question alive, to accept its dramatic nature, because in this poverty that possesses nothing and is not based on acquired frameworks, rituals or safety, I experience the great possibility of perceiving what exists."

3. The criterion of judgement

Taking seriously the urgent need of the human means having in our hands the criterion for judging everything that happens around us, all the positions–ours and of others–, unmasking the deceptions and illusions, and recognizing what is of value. The ultimate and constitutive questions, these "intelligent, dramatic emotions"[22] at the depths of our 'I' represent the point with which we compare every proposal, outlook and encounter.

Ungaretti wrote in one of his poems, "My heart / today / is nothing but / a beat of longing."[23] Etty Hillesum echoed his sentiment. "I always felt that painful insatiable desire, that longing for something

---

[21] F. Varillon, *L'umiltà di Dio* [The humility of God] (Magnano (Bi): Qiqajon–Comunità di Bose, 1999), 30. Our translation from the Italian.

[22] L. Giussani, *The Religious Sense*, 46.

[23] G. Ungaretti, "Oggi" in Id., *Poesie e prose liriche* [Poems and lyrical prose]. *1915-1920* (Milan: Mondadori, 1989), 40. Our translation.

that seemed unattainable to me."[24] We harbor within us a mysterious and inextinguishable longing, like an invisible, unknowable background with which we compare all of life and all our relationships. Saint Augustine calls it restlessness. "For Thou has made us for Thyself and our hearts are restless till they rest in Thee."[25] That restlessness becomes the criterion of judgement for perceiving what his heart is made for. He cannot err, because he can verify it in his experience: rest. That which responds to his restlessness, to his expectant awaiting, is recognizable by the rest he experiences when he encounters it, a rest that safeguards and exalts the expectant awaiting.[26]

Regardless of their place of birth and the culture that welcomed them, all people come into the world with an urgent need for meaning, destiny, and the absolute; at a certain point this need emerges in them and they are forced to face it whether they like it or not, no matter what position they hold. This urgent need may have been buried under the detritus of distraction, but events like the pandemic break through the incrustations, shake us out of our torpor and make the need emerge, keeping us from settling for just any response. Challenged by what happens, we feel this

---

[24] E. Hillesum, "Amsterdam, 16 marzo 1941," in Id., *Diario. Edizione integrale* [Journal. Unabridged edition] (Milan: Adelphi, 2012), 58. Our translation from the Italian.

[25] "*Fecisti nos ad te [Domine] et irrequietum est cor nostrum, donec requiescat in te.*" Saint Augustine, *The Confessions of Saint Augustine,* I,1,1, trans. F.J. Sheed (London: Seed & Ward, Inc., 1942), 3.

[26] Guardini writes, "This 'rest' is something much greater than simply sitting and doing nothing: it is a fullness in oneself." R. Guardini, *Lettere sull'autoformazione* [Letters on self-directed learning] (Brescia: Morcelliana, 1994), 136. Our translation.

urgent need intensify. The more sharply it is felt, the more the response to it leaps before our eyes as the thing that can face it and correspond to it.

So let's try to consider the different positions that we have seen follow one after the other or intertwine in response to the challenge in which we are immersed, in which we can be present entirely or in part, and let's sift and weigh their worth.

a) "Everything's going to be alright"

The most common slogan during the first lockdown was "Everything's going to be alright." In fact, we all face life with a kind of natural hope. We saw it in action as soon as the healthcare crisis began. While doctors and nurses made great and generous efforts, risking their own lives, many people went out on their balconies to manifest their trust. We often heard these words echoing: "Everything's going to be alright." Has this hope, this optimism stood up to the harshness and duration of the challenge? In the second wave it was hard pressed, and we saw how fragile it was, unable to resist the tsunami that overwhelmed it.[27]

The same thing happens in front of the various contradictions that accompany our existence. Leopardi

---

[27] Jean Daniélou points out, "Hope is not optimism. Optimism is the easy attitude by which we think that things will always work out by themselves. In a more reflective form, it considers evil as a simple disorder that will be eliminated by itself, or like growing pains. By voiding the tragic nature of evil, optimism is the worst enemy of hope." J. Daniélou, *Saggio sul mistero della storia* [Essay on the mystery of history] (Brescia: Morcelliana, 2012), 370. Our translation from the Italian translation.

expressed it in a masterful way. "But if a discordant / note assails the ear, / that heaven turns to nothing in an instant."[28] A mere nothing, a discordant note, suffices to threaten the paradise we have built for ourselves. Just imagine what happens when instead there is Covid, with all the consequences we know so well.

The impact with a contradictory circumstance, with a hard reality, tries and questions the substance of our hope. A university student wrote me, "I've always been certain of the presence of a hope and the greatness of the circumstance we are living; all this was clear to me in the first lockdown and above all this summer, when I had to make up for my missed internship. And yet in the recent days a great weight has born down on my heart. My days are no longer dominated by hope, but only by great weariness, abandoned to a thousand daily thoughts and temptations. How can this be?"

b) Solidarity

When an event is "an affair of everyone" as Camus recounted in *The Plague*, each person tries to face it as he or she can. Sooner or later the illusions with which they tried to escape it fall one after another. The cruelty of certain events shakes us so badly that even our most substantial certainties vacillate, like those of Father Paneloux, in Camus's novel, who,

[28] G. Leopardi, "Sopra il ritratto di una bella donna [On the Portrait of a Beautiful Woman, Carved on Her Monument]" vv. 47-49, in *Canti, A Bilingual Edition,* trans. Jonathan Galassi (New York: Farrar, Straus and Giroux, 2012), 257

in front of the death of an innocent, sees the idea of retributive justice collapse. "So then, what is to be done?" writes Recalcati. "Here, the words of the priest [Paneloux] illuminate the assumption of every human experience of care. He tells how during the great plague of Marseilles, of the eighty-one religious in the Convent of Mercy, only four survived. And of these four, three fled to save their lives. But at least one was capable of remaining. This is the last word the priest gives his faithful: to be among those who remain. Knowing how to remain is effectively the first name of every practice of care. It means responding to the appeal of those who have fallen. In biblical terms it is what illuminates the expression 'Here I am!' that makes human care human, not abandoning anyone to the unacceptable violence of evil. Not giving meaning to evil but staying next to those who are struck by it."[29]

As Pope Francis said, Covid has made us more aware of being in the same boat, and this has encouraged many to roll up their sleeves and help out as best they can. Nobody can deny the incomparable value of that effort, but at the same time nobody can affirm that the care given, when it is successful and when it is not, is sufficient for facing the question that arises in the most extreme circumstances: we need not only assistance and medical care, but also something that enables us to look at suffering and death without collapsing in front of it. Here emerges the limit of every attempt, however indispensable,

[29] M. Recalcati, "Ed io avrò cura di te [And I'll Take Care of You]," *la Repubblica*, October 15, 2020, p. 27.

at solidarity, at closeness and care. The nature of the need that the situation has caused to emerge in those who have allowed themselves to be wounded by what was happening is deeper than the response of solidarity.[30]

c) The vaccine as panacea

Welcome vaccines! Who would not rejoice, after having seen so much suffering, fear, bewilderment and death? However, we cannot ignore what Susanna Tamaro wrote in a "Letter to Baby Jesus" published in the Italian newspaper *Corriere della Sera* on December 22, "Forgive us for being convinced that the vaccine will be our salvation, because the vaccine is a marvelous, indispensable help, as is the science at the service of humankind, but it will not be able to dispel the fog of our unhappiness. To do this, we will need a new gaze and a purified heart that will dialogue with it."[31] These words uncover a question we cannot avoid. Is the vaccine enough for answering the questions reawakened by the pandemic? Is this all we need, the eradication of the disease?

---

[30] The same thing happens when we work to respond to the needs of the other: "It is the discovery of the fact that precisely because we love them, *it is not we who make them happy;* and that not even the most perfect society, the most farsighted and legally solid organization, the greatest wealth, the most robust health, the purest beauty, the most civilized culture will ever be able to make them happy." Cf. L. Giussani, *The Meaning of Charitable Work*, http://us.clonline.org/detail.asp?c=5&p=0&id=1663.

[31] S. Tamaro, "Sotto l'albero vorrei ritrovare l'innocenza [Under the Christmas tree I want to find innocence]," *Corriere della Sera*, December 22, 2020, p. 29.

And when there is no cure for a disease? A mother whose child suffers from a very grave syndrome wrote, "In this particularly wearying period my son was hospitalized in intensive care, sedated and intubated. In moments like this, I grab onto anything that makes me remember I am looked upon and loved, and so I call and message my friends, read and reread some things, seeking strength. In this pediatric ward the Internet and telephone service are very poor and because of Covid restrictions I can't see anyone, so the things I usually cling to are unavailable. I remember having read a line, one of the many ones written in the newspapers, 'This past year should be left behind and forgotten. Let's look ahead; the hope of a vaccine is coming.' How can anybody think that hope lies entirely in the vaccine? I think of my son: is being healthy what gives us hope? If so, he would be a goner, and yet instead very often he is the one who testifies to me an immensely greater hope. Looking at him and looking at his body makes me conscious of the desire for good that each of us has, the desire to be happy and loved notwithstanding our defects, which are the drama that make us ask, that enable us to ask for and desire for more."

How can we respond to the abyss that has emerged, but was not caused, by the healthcare emergency? Even before that, what abyss are we talking about? It is the abyss of our own human needs, of the thirst for life we have within. It is also the abyss of the fear of death and pain, which has become more continual, of the anguish of losing life or that life will not be fulfilled definitively. Can the "answers" we have noted fill that abyss?

4. Running away from yourself

A young doctor wrote me, "Initially my approach to the days was to hope that things would go more or less the way I had in mind. I'm a doctor; I finished my specialization in November, and in January moved to a new city to begin a new job. I was full of expectations, with the desire to achieve my vocation as doctor after years of training. In March last year during the first lockdown, the healthcare management was on its knees; my contract lost all priority and I couldn't stay in the hospital any more. I couldn't even stay to give a hand. A useless doctor. In the midst of a pandemic! In the meantime I ran through all the requests for doctors on TV and sent out at least ten resumes responding to offers near and far, but I didn't have the requisites. A useless doctor. You can imagine my anger and frustration. I've always shared what I heard about the value of the unforeseen, but the truth was that deep down I thought that the unforeseen had to fit into the limits I had in mind. So I felt abandoned, rejected, set aside. I said to myself, 'Where is your God? If He exists, He has forgotten you. He probably doesn't exist.' The difficulties of those months left their mark. But I don't want my "Covid crisis" to be squandered; I don't want to miss the opportunity to explore fully the doubt about the existence of God or, on the contrary, the possibility that God exists and truly has my life at heart. Is it possible to affirm with certainty of experience that 'even the hairs of your head are counted'? Is it possible to be so certain that you can explain it to unbelievers or more simply to yourself when you doubt?"

If we do not want to "squander" the crisis we are going through, as Pope Francis said, we cannot miss the opportunity to let ourselves be provoked by the questions that burn inside us. Not squandering the crisis means trying to respond to the doubt that so often pervades us all the way down to the heart. If we do not face it head on and fail to find an answer worthy of the question, we are forced to run away from ourselves, because we find it impossible to stay in front of the drama.

Running away from yourself is the most common road, as long as you can do so, staying far from the abyss of the heart, from the needs that are "impossible" to satisfy, that we cannot tame and that make us restless.

While fear and solidarity in some way dominated the first wave, in the second, as we have said, uncertainty about the future became prevalent, a more acute consciousness of the need for meaning and of the difficulty of staying in front of it. This is the reason for running away. We run away because we cannot stand a life that cries out the need for meaning, and so we try to go as far as possible from ourselves, almost "as if we deemed ourselves less important than all the rest."[32] The price that one pays is a life cut in half, sold short. As Alessandro Baricco wrote recently, "When are we going to talk about this other death? The slithering death that we don't see. There are no government

---

[32] Nicola Cabasilas writes, "What we do, what is habitual for us, what seems right to us, all this is very important for us. It's just that those things that are truly ours, we consider less than all the others, not reflecting on the way to safeguard them and to ensure our right through them, as if we deemed ourselves less important than all the rest. If we do nothing else, let's convert because of that newness that has overturned and transformed all things." N. Cabasilas, *La vita in Cristo* [Life in Christ] (Roma: Città Nuova, 1994), 291.

Covid regulations that take it into account; there are no daily graphs. Officially it doesn't exist. But every day, for a year now, it's been there: all the life that we don't live."[33]

Running away from ourselves, we only worsen the situation because in this way nothing is our own any more: everything becomes extraneous to us. Giussani described it with unforgettable features. "The supreme obstacle on our human journey is the 'neglect' of the 'I,' whereas the first step on a truly human journey–concern for our 'I'–is the exact opposite of that 'neglect'." He continued, "It might seem obvious that one should have this interest, but in fact it is not obvious at all: just think of all those gaping voids that open up in the daily fabric of our consciousness and our frequent distraction." If these words from 1995 seem written for us today, it is because the pandemic has brought to the fore a dynamic of experience that preceded it and will follow it. Giussani's words make us aware of a permanent possibility of the human soul, of a temptation that accompanies us every day: neglect of oneself. "The word 'I' hides great confusion today and yet […] if I neglect my 'I,' it will be impossible for my relationships with life to be my own, for life itself (the sky, a woman, a friend, music) to be mine. To be able to say the word *my* in a serious way, we must have a clear perception of the constitution of our own 'I'. Nothing is as fascinating as the discovery of the real dimen-

[33] A. Baricco, "Mai più, prima puntata [Never again, the first episode]," *www.ilpost.it*, March 9, 2021.

sions of our own 'I.' Nothing is as full of surprises as the discovery of our own human face."[34]

In the spread of this confusion, there is also an influence external to our person. The weakening of the sense of the "I" appears as a symptom of the direction pursued by our culture and of the stall in which it finds itself. "In fact, the evolution of a civilization is such to the degree to which the emergence and clarification of the value of the individual 'I' is promoted." This is the paradoxical outcome of the parabola of modernity, in which the "I" demanded centrality as the master of itself and of things, and reason appointed itself as the measure of reality. God, the Mystery, to whom reality in the final analysis irreducibly points, was expunged from the conception of life and of the world. This did not lead to a closer and more direct relationship with reality, but on the contrary, a flight from it, from its meaning, and to the reduction of human existence to a mere given fact. "In the confusion about the ultimate face of one's own 'I' and of reality, today there is an extreme attempt to continue this flight from the relationship with that infinite Mystery that every reasonable person sees on the horizon and at the root of all human experience: it is necessary to negate any ultimate substance to living. If reality seems to elude man's claim to lordship, the extreme resource of pride is to deny that reality has any substance, to arbitrarily consider everything an illusion or game.

[34] L. Giussani, *The Neglect of the "I"*, excerpt translated from *Alla ricerca del volto umano* (Milan: Bur, 2007), 9, available at https://english.clonline.org/archive/altro/the-neglect-of-the-i.

We can use the term nihilism for what reigns today in the way of thinking and looking."[35]

This flight is described in the Bible in entirely different terms in the first chapter of the book of the prophet Jonah. We know how the story goes. Twice the chapter repeats, "He was fleeing from the Lord."[36] But this flight from God, Giussani says, coincides with "the flight from our responsibility, that is, the flight from 'one' life, from unity with all things, the flight from fullness, the flight from meaning and fullness." Therefore, even if we were "decidedly devoted to a Catholic movement," as he said in 1963 to a group of CL leaders, and even if we gave all our free time to it, the flight from the relationship with the Mystery "is an emptiness that we allow for every one of our days."[37] It is a flight from oneself that can take on different forms.

a) Activism

We can avoid the cry that comes from the innermost depths of our humanity by throwing ourselves frenetically into action, getting so involved that we have no time for thinking about our true needs. Activity becomes like a drug. We saw how much this activism invades our life when the lockdown forced us to stop: closed in at home, we were suddenly forced to deal

[35] *Ibid. Alla Ricerca del volto umano*, 10, 13. Our translation.
[36] Cf. Jonah 1:10.
[37] Fraternità di Comunione e Liberazione, *Documentazione audiovisiva* [Audiovisual documentation], Esercizi Incaricati di GS [Spiritual Exercises for GS Leaders], Varigotti (SV), December 6-9, 1963.

with ourselves. So many of us discovered themselves to be empty and disoriented, and could not bear to look at themselves! Activism is a way of operating without an adequate reason, and thus it does not open us or cause us to mature. In this way, when we are forced to pause, we feel full of insecurity and sense our own weight like a mountain on our shoulders. A young woman wrote me, "In these difficult and arid months, I've come to see that I cannot stay in front of certain questions and when they emerge, something that happens often, I try to bury them with a list of things to do, because I have no answer. This destroys me. When my friends ask how I'm doing, I never know what to say. I have two fantastic, healthy children. We're all well, and haven't suffered economically from the pandemic. I don't have anything to complain about, but I always feel a great emptiness and solitude. I'm always angry and always see the negative side of everything. I'm almost never free with my friends because I'm afraid that if I talk about this emptiness it'll create an embarrassing silence with no way out but a quick change of subject."

The activism of which I speak can have many objects or spheres: normally it is work, but it can be a political party or a cultural association, volunteer work, or, as Fr. Giussani said, a "Catholic movement." We are the first to participate in this attitude: we can avoid a serious engagement with our humanity by focusing on things to do. Even "doing things of the Movement" can be a way of running away from ourselves.

On many occasions Giussani warned us about this attitude, pointing to what is hidden at its roots. In fact, in activism, the things we do and are involved in and in which we seek satisfaction constitute the effective meaning of living and the true object of esteem: not God, Christ, the relationship with the Mystery made flesh. "Existentially, we hold other things in greater esteem than Christ." We are bound to the Movement not for the Mystery it carries, but for the things we do, and "this does not develop the experience of our life."[38] We do not consider it exaggerated to say these things. In fact, when what binds us is only the things we do, sooner or later our being together loses interest. "I abandoned the Movement thirty years ago, at the end of university: my days were full of activity and relationships, but the meaning of everything was lost, taken for granted and thus life was arid."

b) Distraction, to fill the emptiness with noise

When it becomes almost inevitable to gain awareness of our own fragility, as happened in this period of provocations and trials, when we touch our own ephemeral and contingent nature, we easily turn to the weapon of distraction. When questions arise that undermine our certainties, that disturb us and that we do not know how to answer, we fill the empty lack of an answer with noise. In our free time we pursue stimuli and news, we wander here and there on the Internet and social networks, we find a series of new interests, we pass quickly from one thing to another without looking deeply at anything: our objective, confessed or unconfessed, is

[38] L. Giussani, *La convenienza umana della fede* [Why Faith is Humanly Worthwhile] (Milan: Bur, 2018), 104 and 107. Our translation.

to elude the question of destiny, the urgent need we feel, to try to avoid dealing with ourselves.[39] We know it is destined to fail in the end, but we settle for the short term respite it allows us.

Distraction and the lack of reflection can characterize many of our days, and even long periods of our life. In a certain sense, they are the other face of cynicism. In fact, when activism does not work cynicism enters in as another way to close the door on the urgent need, preferring to brand everything as lacking substance and sail "along the shore of the sentiment of nothingness."[40]

Bernanos confessed, "I did not believe that what is defined with such a common word as distraction could have such a character of dissociation and crumbling."[41] Our person sinks into alienation and the mechanism; we become less and less present to ourselves. Being distracted means being ripped away from the substance of living.

c) *The return to normalcy, to turn the page*

"What's ahead of us? Is the game really up? Can we get back to the life we used to live, or is it gone for-

---

[39] As Romano Guardini notes, "distraction is the state in which man has neither a center, nor unity; his thoughts wander from one object to another, his feeling is indeterminate and his will is not master of his own possibilities." R. Guardini, *Introduzione alla preghiera* [Introduction to Prayer] (Brescia: Morcelliana, 1973), 23.

[40] L. Giussani, *La familiarità con Cristo* [Familiarity with Christ] (Cinisello Balsamo (Mi): San Paolo, 2008), 147.

[41] G. Bernanos, *Diario di un curato di campagna* [Diary of A Country Priest] (Milan, Mondadori, 1967), 238-239. Our translation.

ever?"[42] Orwell asked himself in 1939. The question has not lost its bite. Turn the page as soon as possible, leave behind what has happened, forget! This is the imperative that seems to be circulating, to act as if nothing had happened, as if the questions had not been reawakened, all those people had not died and the bewilderment had only been an incident that can be wiped away. This temptation is very real and present, as Vasilij Grossman wrote at the end of his life. "That everything return to the way it was before that unbearable change, that everything return to being habit, something well known, and that there remain no trace of the newness that breaks your bones and enters into your blood…"[43] Such an attitude will never be the wellspring for a gain for our experience. Rather, the opposite is evident.

---

[42] G. Orwell, *Coming Up For Air,* http://gutenberg.net.au/ebooks02/0200031h. html

[43] V. Grossman, *Il bene sia con voi!* [Blessing to you!] (Milan: Adelphi, 2011), 212. Our translation.

CHAPTER 2

WE *ARE* EXPECTANT AWAITING

Activism, distraction, the demand to return to normalcy–not, let's be clear, the understandable need to overcome the difficulties and reach a more sustainable healthcare and economic situation, but the anxiety to forget, to silence the human questions–these are all ways of running away from yourself and reality. For most people, they are habitual, and enable them not to deal with that depth of their own "I" that we can summarize with the expression already used, "expectant awaiting" for life, meaning, fullness, and fulfillment. However, as we have said, there are situations like the pandemic and all its consequences that even just for a few moments jerk us out of our distraction, stop us in our flight, and set us in front of ourselves.

Why do our efforts to achieve fulfillment or run from ourselves fail? Because "the soul exceeds the world; it is not satisfied with what the eyes see, with what I know. It cries with longing."[1] No matter how hard or stubbornly we try, none of our attempts can achieve the fulfillment that we seek implicitly or explicitly when we rise in the morning, when we undertake our activities or organize our "evasions." Because of the structural

---

[1] P. Van der Meer, *Diario di un convertito* [Diary of a Convert] (Alba (Cn): Paoline, 1967), 34. Our translation.

insufficiency of our strength and things that we may even manage to obtain, we are unable to find what we expectantly await, deep down. For this reason, Simone Weil noted acutely, "The most precious things need not be sought; we should just wait for them expectantly. In fact, people cannot find them with their own strength alone, and if they set out to seek them, they will find in their place false goods whose falseness they will not even be able to recognize."[2]

1. An ineradicable fact

Thus expectant awaiting is what always remains when our attempts, including the successful ones–actually, I'd say, above all the successful ones–have proven insufficient to reach the goal, that is, self-fulfillment, fullness here and now in every moment, not tomorrow or in the next world.

One of the greatest contemporary poets, recently deceased, Adam Zagajewski, captured with these words the vastness of our expectant awaiting:
"Those brief instants
That happen so rarely–
Is this life?
Those few days
When clarity returns–
Is this life?
Those moments when music
Reacquires its own dignity–

---

[2] S. Weil, *Attesa di Dio* [Waiting for God] (Milan: Rusconi, 1972), 76. Our translation from the Italian translation.

Is this life?
Those rare hours
When love triumph–
Is this life?"[3]

The poem voices beautifully something that belongs to everyone's experience. Even though the culture in which we live tries to suppress this expectancy, to discourage or change it, all its attempts clash with something it cannot avoid: our human nature. Bertold Brecht acknowledges this in one of his poems:

"Not fulfillment of desire but forgetfulness
Passes for wisdom.
I can do none of this:
Indeed I live in the dark ages!"[4]

Not even the dark ages can uproot desire from the heart, this expectant awaiting for something that corresponds to our thirst for life. "The dominant culture," which can have a certain self-interest in emptying life of meaning and promoting existential nihilism, "no matter how much it can occupy the mind of the individual and thus of the masses, faces a limit that forces it to stop: human nature, which is defined by the religious sense." This nature, Giussani says, "not only will never be completely atrophied, but will always be in a more or less perceptible position of expectant awaiting.[5]

[3] A. Zagajewski, "I brevi istanti [The fleeting moments]", in Id., *Guarire dal silenzio* (Milan: Mondadori, 2020), 16. Our translation from the Italian translation.

[4] B. Brecht, "To Posterity," vv. 30-33. trans. H.R. Hays, https://allpoetry.com/To-Posterity

[5] L. Giussani, *Un avvenimento di vita, cioè una storia* [A Life Event, i.e. a History], edited by C. Di Martino (Rome: EDIT, 1993), 41. Our translation.

This expectant awaiting is an ineradicable fact that each of us deals with in every moment of living, even when we run from it. "Has anyone ever promised us anything? Then why should we expect anything?"[6] With these words Pavese identified the center of his and our "I," something that belongs to all of us: expectant awaiting. It belongs to our original fabric: we are made as "expectant awaiting for." Not only do we await: we *are* expectant awaiting!

A friend wrote me, "I find that my deepest 'I' expectantly awaits something that will give it hope and enable it to say 'Yes, there is hope.' In a moment when I would be led to respond, 'Well, I'm not so sure about it,' I become aware that I am made up of the expectancy that everything I live is ultimately positive; in other words, I'm made for hope. I know that many times both Giussani and you have told and shown us that if this expectant awaiting exists, then this already is a sign that there is something that responds to it. But it seems to me that I only repeat this in words, not experience."

Everyone, even those who seem extraneous to this expectant awaiting, who give it no weight or do not take it seriously, caught up in distractions or censorship of their own humanity, when they come up against a presence charged with a promise, a meaning that has to do with it, do not remain indifferent: they see this expectancy kindle in themselves, and have to confess to themselves that they too secretly were awaiting it. This was the case for the university

---

[6] C. Pavese, *This Business of Living: Diaries 1935-1950* (London and New York: Routledge, 2017), 267.

students who, in the interval between one lockdown and another, in a climate of almost total acquiescence, received from some fellow students the flyer entitled, "The university is not closed as long as we live."[7] Their face changed: expectant awaiting resurfaced in them.

Expectant awaiting is a fact, as Benedict XVI reminded us. "Expectation or waiting is a dimension that flows through our whole personal, family and social existence. Expectation is present in thousands of situations, from the smallest and most banal to the most important that involve us completely and in our depths. Among these, let us think of waiting for a child, on the part of a husband and wife; of waiting for a relative or friend who is coming from far away to visit us; let us think, for a young person, of waiting to know his results in a crucially important examination or of the outcome of a job interview; in emotional relationships, of waiting to meet the beloved, of waiting for the answer to a letter, or for the acceptance of forgiveness... One could say that man is alive as long as he waits, as long as hope is alive in his heart. And from his expectations man recognizes himself: our moral and spiritual 'stature' can be measured by what we wait for, by what we hope for."[8]

Expectant awaiting is so constitutive of our "I" that not even the ugliest, most painful, most contradictory situations can eliminate it entirely; even in circumstances where there would be every reason to give up

[7] https://www.ateneostudenti.it/2020/11/01/luniversita-non-e-chiusa-finche-noi-viviamo/
[8] Benedict XVI, *Angelus*, November 28, 2010. http://www.vatican.va/content/benedict-xvi/en/angelus/2010/documents/hf_ben-xvi_ang_20101128.html

this expectancy, we have testimony of it. "My time is always full, but from the morning to the evening, deep down, there is expectancy,"[9] wrote Dietrich Bonhoeffer from the Berlin prison of Tegel, where he was jailed from 1943 to 1945 and then hung, because of his opposition to the Nazi regime. He did not waste a minute, and in the background his expectancy grew.

Nothing can defeat this elementary and indestructible evidence: we are "expectant awaiting for." Alluding to a Kafka short story, the Spanish writer Gustavo Martín Garzo spoke of our heart that awaits like "an animal that asks for things we are unable to do, but insists that we do them."[10]And Iribarren, in the same direction, writes, "And how can it be / –I say to myself, watching life passing toward / the beach–, that notwithstanding / the merciless devastations that time inflicts on us / there is not the slightest attenuation / not a second's truce / in this incessant dream of the impossible."[11]

2. Affection for oneself

But pay attention here, because the fact of this expectant awaiting, even while it is powerful and objective,

[9] D. Bonhoeffer, *Resistenza e resa* [Resistance and Surrender] (Brescia: Queriniana, 2002), 146. Our translation from the Italian translation.

[10] G.M. Garzo, "Estimado Franz Kafka," *El País*, October 25, 2020. Our translation from the Italian translation.

[11] "Y cómo puede ser / –me digo, viendo pasar la vida / hacia la playa–, que, pese / a las devastaciones inclementes / que el tiempo / nos inflige, / no se amortigüe un ápice / siquiera, no nos dé tregua / un segundo, / este incesante / soñar con lo imposible." K.C. Iribarren, "Verano cruel," in Id., *Seguro que esta historia te suena*, 330-331. Our translation from the Italian translation.

does not have the last word. It demands to be acknowledged, accepted and made to count. Therefore it challenges our reason and freedom. This is our greatness as human beings: expectant awaiting is in our nature but as I said, we can try in all sorts of ways to live as if it did not exist, distracting ourselves, pretending that it does not exist. It exists, but it does not impose itself automatically.

We must acknowledge the evidence that we are *made of* expectant awaiting; it does not automatically impose itself. Some might view this as just one more in a long series of misfortunes. They might also view in the same light the fact that our own efforts cannot satisfy this expectant awaiting, nor can we eliminate it. But if we remain faithful to our experience, we understand that it is not in our best interests at all to rip it out of the fiber of our being, and it is fortunate that the attempt to suffocate this expectancy cannot, in the final analysis, be successful. Once again, Pavese is illuminating. "Waiting is still an occupation. It is having nothing to wait for that is terrible."[12] Each of us can verify this when we wake in the morning and expect nothing. In those moments, you can confess to yourself whether it is better to wake up expecting something, or to open your eyes on the day without expecting anything.

Expectant awaiting, which nobody can entirely uproot from the heart, sets us each morning in front of an alternative that calls into play the thing that defines our greatness as human beings: freedom. What is the alternative? Take this expectant awaiting seriously, or

[12] C. Pavese, *This Business of Living: Diaries 1935-1950*, 281.

give up. The decision is never a given. We are free for this. A person wrote me, "This is the first time I've tried to respond to the questions you ask us before the Spiritual Exercises or assemblies, because it's the first time I've taken myself so seriously as to tell myself that the question 'Is there hope?' is aimed right at me, and that it's not just up to the 'others' to respond. I've discovered that I am the protagonist in my life."

The drama of our freedom, which comes into play every day, is well described by "George Gray" in the *Spoon River Anthology*:

"I have studied many times
The marble which was chiseled for me–
A boat with a furled sail at rest in a harbor.
In truth it pictures not my destination
But my life.
For love was offered me and I shrank from its
                             disillusionment;
Sorrow knocked at my door, but I was afraid;
Ambition called to me, but I dreaded the chances.
Yet all the while I hungered for meaning in my life.
And now I know that we must lift the sail
And catch the winds of destiny
Wherever they drive the boat.
To put meaning in one's life may end in madness,
But life without meaning is the torture
Of restlessness and vague desire–
It is a boat longing for the sea and yet afraid.[13]

We are like a boat longing for the sea; it cannot fail to expect it because this longing is constitutive, and

---

[13] E. Lee Masters, "George Gray," in *Spoon River Anthology*, public domain, available at https://poets.org/poem/george-gray

yet it fears it. Here, then, is the battle: either to respond to the longing for the sea, the hunger for a life full of meaning, or to withdraw, settle, and choose not to risk, out of fear of unforeseeable possibilities.

This temptation to withdraw from our humanity, to spare ourselves unforeseeable possibilities out of fear, remaining safe "at rest in a harbor" aboard a "boat with a furled sail" is what Jesus was talking about in the Gospel with His parable of the talents.

"It will be as when a man who was going on a journey called in his servants and entrusted his possessions to them. To one he gave five talents; to another, two; to a third, one—to each according to his ability. Then he went away. Immediately the one who received five talents went and traded with them, and made another five. Likewise, the one who received two made another two. But the man who received one went off and dug a hole in the ground and buried his master's money. After a long time the master of those servants came back and settled accounts with them. The one who had received five talents came forward bringing the additional five. He said, 'Master, you gave me five talents. See, I have made five more.' His master said to him, 'Well done, my good and faithful servant. Since you were faithful in small matters, I will give you great responsibilities. Come, share your master's joy.' [Then] the one who had received two talents also came forward and said, 'Master, you gave me two talents. See, I have made two more.' His master said to him, 'Well done, my good and faithful servant. Since you were faithful in small matters, I will give you great responsibilities. Come, share your master's joy.' Then the one who had received the one talent came forward and said, 'Master, I knew you were a demanding person, harvesting where you did not plant and gathering where you did not scatter; so out of fear I went off and buried your talent in the ground. Here it is back.' His master said to him in reply, 'You wicked, lazy servant! So you knew that I harvest where I did not plant and gather where I did not scatter? Should you not then have put my money in the bank so that I could have got it back with interest on my return? Now then! Take the talent from him and give it to the one with ten. For to everyone who has, more will be given and he will grow rich; but from the one who has not, even what he has will be taken away. And throw this useless servant into the darkness outside, where there will be wailing and grinding of teeth'."[14]

The master berates the servant who, out of fear, chose not to risk. Jesus says that only those who risk can gain life. In fact, the parable ends with the words, "For to everyone who has, more will be given and he will grow rich; but from the one who has not, even what he has will be taken away." Jesus well knew human nature and the temptation not to risk, to pull in the oars, remaining comfortably in the harbor. But those who risk nothing in life, who do not throw themselves into life to earn meaning, will remain with nothing, empty.

Taking seriously your need, your hunger and thirst for a full life is the first sign of affection for yourself, but this affection is not at all a given for most people. In fact, "we necessarily feel" demands or needs "and we lament with a cry of pain […] when they are not

[14] Mt 25:14-30.

satisfied, but normally we do not take them seriously."[15] We do not recognize their importance, or follow
the direction they indicate.

What is needed in order to have this affection for
yourself that enables you to take seriously your own
longing, your own need? "Affection for yourself demands poverty," Giussani said to university students
in 1983. "This is why Christ said, 'Blessed are the poor
in spirit,' or 'Blessed are those who hunger and thirst
for justice,' because [affection for yourself] is not the
attachment to something that we have defined ourselves, but to something that defines us; the acknowledgment of something that defines us, without our
having been able to intervene to determine the question. Thus the need for love or the need for personal
realization or the need for companionship is something incomparably greater and deeper. We should
listen to these needs and pay attention to them with
all seriousness, a far different matter from all the furi-
ous tenacity we invest in wanting the objects we have
thought, imagined or chosen."[16]

Thus affection for yourself has nothing to do with
self-love: it opens us to the discovery of our constitutive demands, our original needs, in their nakedness and vastness. In fact, who are the poor in spirit?
"Those who have nothing except one thing for which
and by which they are made, in other words, boundless aspiration [...]; limitless expectant awaiting. It is
not boundless because the heap of things expected

---

[15] L. Giussani, *Uomini senza patria (1982-1983)* [Men Without a Homeland]
(Milan: Bur, 2008), 295. Our translation.
[16] *Ibid.*, p. 296.

is limitless; no [those who are poor in spirit] expect nothing [concrete, which would then disappoint], but live a boundless openness […] [this almost seems like a contradiction]. As said in a poem by Clemente Rebora […]: 'I'm not expecting anyone…,' and yet […] he is there, stretching out toward it."[17] This is the originality of human beings, being stretched out toward something they do not yet know, but that seizes them from head to foot.

The human person is expectant awaiting. This is our nature. But expectancy for what? The human heart is expectant awaiting for the infinite, a boundless expectancy. The poor in spirit live this expectant awaiting, stretching out toward something they do not know and do not measure, but that constitutes them and attracts them irresistibly.

It is not easy to meet people who grasp the human in its totality, without reductions. I still remember how impressed I was, listening to Giussani. He looked at the human with such capacity for embracing everything of which it is made, that I wanted to embrace myself in the same way. It filled me with gratitude to know that there was someone who embraced my humanity so radically. When we meet someone with a similar gaze, it is a liberation. Giussani continued, "The seriousness of affection for yourself is the perception of your own boundless need, but, and I insist, not of your boundless need because you want a hundred thousand things and then you desire a hundred thousand and one! It is boundless because it has no pre-es-

17 *Ibid.*, p. 298.

tablished image of the things it needs: 'It is' need!".[18]
It is expectant awaiting! Who knows what experience
must be lived, to be able to say these things! Each of
us "is" need, a boundless need, before and beyond any
possible image.

3. "Oh, that You would rend the heavens and come down"

Taking seriously this expectant awaiting does not less-
en trepidation about what will fulfill it, a trepidation
that is seen in ourselves and has been seen throughout
history: within us we have an irreducible and unique
expectancy that is boundless, and it is not in our power to imagine what will fulfill it. It is a mystery. This
expectant awaiting is directed toward "something"
that we do not know, that surpasses any identification
or measure. This is hard to accept, but the greatness of
the human person is all here.

Since I first read it in Leopardi, I have never forgotten his affirmation that "the inability to be satisfied by
any worldly thing"[19] is the chief sign of the greatness

---

[18] *Ibid.*, p. 299.

[19] Here is the well-known passage, in its entirety: This "inability to be satisfied by any worldly thing or so to speak, by the entire world. To consider the
inestimable amplitude of space, the number of worlds, and their astonishing
size, then to discover that all this is small and insignificant compared to the
capacity of one's own mind; to imagine the infinite number of worlds, the
infinite universe, then to feel that our mind and aspirations might be even
greater than such a universe; to accuse things always of being inadequate and
meaningless; to suffer want, emptiness, and hence boredom–this seems to
me the chief sign of the grandeur and nobility of human nature." G. Leopardi, *Pensieri, LXVIII*, trans. W.S. Di Piero (Baton Rouge and London: Louisi-
ana State University Press, 1981), 113.

of the human person. Such a gaze upon the human person is rare. For many, the inability to be satisfied by any earthly thing is a terrible misfortune, and they would do anything to reduce this expectant awaiting in order to settle for something within reach. On the contrary, Miguel de Unamuno wrote, "what is only transitory does not satisfy me, in my longing for eternity, and […] without it I am indifferent to everything else and everything else makes no difference to me. I need it, I really do! Without it there is no more joy in life and life joys have nothing to tell me anymore. It is just too easy to say: 'You just have to live and be content with life.' And what about those who are not content?"[20]

This lack of satisfaction points to something so great as to be unimaginable. "The present situation of the human person is pure expectancy of an event that cannot be prepared for in any way, and whose appearance is absolutely unforeseeable."[21] We do not know what it is or how it will happen, but we wait for it expectantly. In fact, it is what above all, at the bottom of everything, we await supremely, today as then, two thousand years ago.

Ernest Hello, speaking of the time of Jesus, captured it well. "During their wait, the ancient Roman world

[20] M. de Unamuno, *Cartas inéditas de Miguel de Unamuno y Pedro Jiménez Ilundain*, edited by H. Benítez, Revista de la Universidad de Buenos Aires 3 (9/1949), pp. 135, 150; quoted by Fr. Raniero Cantalamessa, *We proclaim to you eternal life (1Jn. 1:2)*, Second preaching for Advent, December 11, 2020. English translation by Paolo Zanna on http://www.cantalamessa.org/?p=3901&lang=en

[21] J. Daniélou, *Saggio sul mistero della storia* [Essay on the Mystery of History], 216. Our translation from the Italian translation.

had committed enormous abominations; opposing ambitions clashed in wars, and the earth bowed to the scepter of Caesar Augustus. The earth had not yet realized the importance of what was done in her. Stunned by the noise […] of wars and conflicts, she had not yet realized something important that was happening: it was the silence of those who waited in the deep solemnity of desire. The earth knew nothing of all this. If it were all to start again today, she would not know any more than she did then. She would not know it, with the same lack of knowledge; she would distain it with the same distain, if she were forced to become aware of it. The silence, I say, was the true thing that *took place* unknown to her on her surface. This silence was an authentic action. It was not a negative silence, an absence of words. It was a positive silence, active beyond any action. While Octavius and Anthony fought over the empire of the world, Simeon and Anna waited expectantly. Who among them was more active?"[22]

Benedict XVI described the mystery of this expectant awaiting. "In the time before Jesus' birth the expectation of the Messiah was very strong in Israel–that is, the expectation of an Anointed one, a descendent of King David, who would at last set the people [of Israel] free from every form of moral and political slavery and find the Kingdom of God. But no one would ever have imagined that the Messiah could be born of a humble girl like Mary, the betrothed of a righteous man, Joseph. Nor would she have ever thought of it, and yet in her heart the expectation of the Savior was

---

[22] E. Hello, *Fisionomie di Santi* [Figures of Saints] (Turin: "La Torre d'avorio"–Fogola, 1977), 58-59. Our translation from the Italian translation.

so great, her faith and hope were so ardent, that he was able to find in her a worthy mother. Moreover, God himself had prepared her before time. There is a mysterious correspondence between the waiting of God and that of Mary [...], totally transparent to the loving plan of the Most High."[23]

The expectant awaiting found in Simeon, Anna and Mary are not only something of the past. No, in the same silence as then, far from the spotlights as then, that expectant awaiting remains in the innermost depths of our humanity, in the silence of our heart, in the intimate reaches of our "I." And it continues to burn. A university student wrote, "My humanity is constantly expecting a Presence that fulfills it." This is also what Rilke, the great German poet, affirmed: "always distracted by expectation, as though each moment / announced a beloved's coming."[24] The expectation that originally constitutes our heart is for a presence that responds, that saves, safeguards and fulfills our humanity.

As described in Daniele Mencarelli's most recent autobiographic novel, "I would like to tell my mother what I really need, always the same thing, ever since my first wails when I entered the world. What I've wanted for so long has not been easy to say; I tried to explain it with complicated concepts. I spent these first twenty years studying the best words for describing it. I used many words, too many, then I understood that I had to proceed in the opposite direction,

23 Benedict XVI, *Angelus*, November 28, 2010.

24 R.M. Rilke, "First Elegy," vv. 31-32, in *Duino Elegies: A Bilingual Edition*, trans. Edward Snow (New York: North Point Press, 2000), 7.

and so, day by day, I began to eliminate one, the least necessary, superfluous. Bit by bit I shortened, pruned, until I reached one word. One word to say what I truly want, this thing that I have carried with me since my birth, before my birth, that follows me like a shadow, always at my side. Salvation. I do not say this word to anyone else. But there it is, and with that word its meaning, greater than death. Salvation. For me. For my mother on the other end of the line. For all the children and all their mothers. And fathers. And all the siblings of all times, past and future. My sickness is called salvation. What? Who can I say this to?"[25]

At the apex of the arduous and impassioned consciousness of existence, the cry of our humanity explodes like an entreaty that rises from the depths of the heart of people from all time, an invocation to the unfathomable Mystery. "Oh, that You would rend the heavens and come down!"[26] This is the entreaty implicit every time we wake up and in every gesture of the day, even of those who do not know who this 'You' is, even though they also await Him. "That You would rend the heavens and come down!" is the entreaty of the reason and the affection of people who do not want to live in vain. For this reason, Montale, who in his way was familiar with the human, wrote "There's greater joy in waiting."[27]

Since we are expectantly awaiting something without knowing how it will make itself present, the prob-

[25] D. Mencarelli, *Tutto chiede salvezza* [Everything Asks for Salvation] (Milan: Mondadori, 2020), 22-23. Our translation.

[26] Is 63:19.

[27] E. Montale, "Glory of an Expansive Noon," in Montale, *Poems*, trans. Jonathan Galassi (London: Everyman's Library, 2020.)

lem is not one of intelligence, but of attention. This is what we need to ask for, as Pope Francis stressed, quoting Saint Augustine: "'*Timeo Iesum transeuntem*' (*Sermons*, 88, 14, 13), 'I fear that Jesus will pass by me unnoticed.' Caught up in our daily concerns […] and distracted by so many vain things, we risk losing sight of what is essential. This is why today the Lord repeats: '*To all, I say*: be watchful!' (*Mk.* 13:37). Be watchful, attentive."[28]

[28] Francis, *Homily at the Eucharistic Concelebration with the new cardinals*, November 29, 2020.

CHAPTER 3

THE UNEXPECTED LEAP OF THE HEART

The upheavals of the present have shaken up ways of living that we took for granted. "But that was the way with facts. They punctured every bubble of conceit, shattered theories, destroyed convictions."[1] In the face of life and death, many have unexpectedly felt, even if only for a moment, an urgent need for an ultimate meaning, a need we can never entirely keep at bay. It is no surprise that many of the things that previously counted as sure evidence no longer form part of our basic cultural inheritance. As Morin said, uncertainty is the hallmark of our time, but it has been further intensified by the gravity and persistence of the pandemic. No matter what your starting point, it has become difficult to remain anchored to what you consider something already known, to entrust yourself with inertia to the illusion of having life in your power. Paradoxically, maybe it is actually helpful to see certain monolithic assumptions of ours crumble, to experience the beginning of a crack in the wall of our safe beliefs. In the lyrics of Leonard Cohen, "There is a crack, a crack in everything / That's how the light gets in."[2]

---

[1] I.B. Singer, *Enemies, A Love Story* (New York: Farrar, Straus and Giroux, 1998), 166.

[2] "There is a crack, a crack in everything / That's how the light gets in." ("Anthem," lyrics and music by Leonard Cohen from the album, *The Future*, 1992, Columbia Records).

1. "An unexpected event is my only hope. But they say that's asking for trouble."

The duel starts afresh every morning. Each of us can see it when we wake and prepare to face the journey of the day full of expectancy for fulfillment. This is described effectively in a well-known poem by Montale, *Before the Trip*.

"Before the trip we pore over timetables,
connections, stopovers, overnight stays
and reservations (rooms with bath
or shower, one bed or two, even a suite);
we consult
the Guides Hachettes and museums catalogues,
change money, sort francs
from escudos, rubles from kopecks;
before setting out we inform
friends or relatives, check
suitcases and passports,
equipment, buy extra
razor blades, and finally
glance at our wills, pure
knocking-on-wood since the percentage
of plane crashes is nil;
                              before
the trip we're calm while suspecting
that the wise don't travel and the pleasure
of returning is bought at a price.
And then we leave and everything's O.K.
                              and everything's
For the best and pointless.
. . . .
                              And now what about

my journey?
I've arranged it too carefully
without knowing anything about it. An unexpected
                                                    event
is my only hope. But they say
that's asking for trouble." [3]

We can prepare everything for the journey of life, of every day, of every hour, with the various appointments and yet even before knowing how it will go, we can confess to ourselves, "everything is O.K. and pointless." No matter how unaware or distracted we may be, we have some presentiment of the dimension of our expectant awaiting and feel certain in advance that all our preparations will not serve the purpose, will not be able to obtain what we are waiting for, that is, to fulfill the expectancy with which we wake in the morning or begin the journey. Our past experience has taught us this. So we understand why "an unexpected event is my only hope." Something has to happen that is not part of our plans, something that exceeds our preparations and projections. "With all things, it is always what comes to us from outside, freely and by surprise, as a gift from heaven, without our having sought it, that brings us pure joy. In the same way, real good can only come from outside ourselves, never from our own effort. We cannot under any circumstances manufacture something which is better than ourselves."[4]

---

[3] E. Montale, "Before the Trip," in Id., *The Collected Poems of Eugenio Montale, 1925–1977*, trans. William Arrowsmith (New York: W.W. Norton & Company, 2012), 397-399.

[4] S. Weil, *Gravity and Grace*, trans. Arthur Wills (London: Octagon Books, 1983), 94.

That this unexpected event happens is the peak of human expectant awaiting. "But they say / that's asking for trouble," Montale concludes. On the one hand, he calls for this unexpected event as "my only hope," but on the other hand, he denies that it is possible. In fact, "those in the know" say only children or the naïve think this unexpected event can really happen. We, too, often feel the grip of this temptation, and we acquiesce. "Yes, it's asking for trouble." It's foolishness to say so to yourself. But is it true? If we challenge this affirmation, submitting reason to experience, we realize that the one true foolishness is to force reality into the narrow confines of our "already known," thinking that we already know everything, dictating the limits to the possible, and thus not expecting anything.

"I have a sense," Michel Houellebecq has his troubled main character say in his most recent novel, "that even when you plunge into true night, polar night–the one that lasts for six months in a row–the concept or the memory of the sun remains. I had entered an *endless night*, and yet there remained, deep within me, there remained something less than a hope, let's say an uncertainty. One might also say that even when one has personally lost the game, when one has played one's last card, for some people–not all, not all–the idea remains that *something in heaven* will pick up the hand [...], even when one has never at any moment in one's life sensed the intervention or even the presence of any kind of deity, even when one is aware of not especially deserving the intervention of a favourable deity, and even when one realizes, bearing in mind the accumulation of mistakes and errors that constitute one's life, that one deserves it less than anyone."[5]

The one true foolishness is to deny the possibility of the event. Giussani spoke of this as a "crime against the supreme category of reason, of possibility."[6] Though the skeptical position may seem the most rational, it actually is a crime against reason. Nobody can claim that they know everything, dominate everything, can foresee everything that may happen, and exclude the possibility that the unexpected of which Montale spoke might happen. This would be foolishness, indeed! The category of possibility belongs to the nature of reason. Therefore the only truly reasonable position is to leave the possibility open, not only at the beginning but always, now, in any moment of living.

Leaving open the possibility that something may happen that exceeds our capacity for foreseeing is not a renunciation of reason, but actually is living it fully, to its depths, according to its nature and original impetus, a window thrown open to reality, not the measure of the limits. Preventive skepticism toward everything that exceeds our measure is a blockage of reason, not its apex, and influences us more than we think; it enters inside almost without our realizing it.[7]

---

[5] M. Houellebecq, *Serotonin*, trans. Shaun Whiteside (London: William Heinemann, 2019), 270-271.

[6] L. Giussani, *At the Origin of the Christian Claim*, trans. Viviane Hewett (Montreal: McGill-Queen's University Press, 1998), 31.

[7] Vasilij Grossman observes, through a character in his great novel: "I'm beginning to have the sensation that here nothing is left of man, except suspicion." V. Grossman, *Life and Fate*, trans. Robert Chandler (London: Vintage Classics, 2006).

A young friend wrote me, "I'd like to tell you briefly how I've lived this recent period, after having read the question for these Spiritual Exercises: 'Is there hope?'. The song that best describes these months is *Amare ancora [Continue loving]* by Chieffo: "But the bitterness, my love / seeing the things as I see." I've discovered that I don't have the same freshness of my first years at the university. I don't have the same simplicity in my gaze: the skepticism that invades the world has invaded me, too. Very often I feel a strong resistance to saying that God is the one who gives me things and that they are a gift. I look at a beautiful landscape and I see in myself a subtle suspicion about the experience of correspondence I live in front of that beauty. This suspicion hurts me and provokes great sadness: how *bitter* to see things in this way! I feel this bitterness because I've been a witness to and protagonist in another way of looking at reality: the music I study, the sky, the sea, the mountains, trees, everything was acknowledged as a sign of One who prefers me, who affirms me as a unique being, exclusive and unrepeatable in the whole universe. Also, and to my immense pain, I have this same skepticism toward Christ, to He whom I acknowledged present in this companionship. The song continues, "It would be enough just to return to being children and remembering ... / [...] that everything is given, / that everything is new and freed." I experienced this in my first years in the CLU [the university students involved in Communion and Liberation], and truly, it was heaven on earth." And so he asked, "Is there hope that I can return to being like a child, to looking with the same gaze as before? Is it possible to re-educate this gaze, which has become corrupted?"

There is a skepticism that invades us and with it a suspicion that ruins any beauty that presents itself on our journey.[8] The shadow that this suspicion casts on everything beautiful that appears before our eyes is like a curse, and from the innermost depths of the sadness it causes, a question arises. "Is there hope that I can return to being like a child, to looking with the same gaze as before? Is it possible to re-educate this gaze, which has become corrupted?" This is the same question of the elderly scribe Nicodemus, a doctor of the law. "How can a person once grown old be born again?"[9] What a grace to be able to repeat it in a way that is not rhetorical–like a quote among the others, almost as if to paint over our poverty with a coat of culture–discovering it as it gushes from our inner-most depths in all its truth! "How can a person once grown old be born again?"

We often find that we lack openness to possibility, that we are prone to closure, that we easily close and bar the door to what happens. A university student wrote, "In the months before the second wave, how many moments were thrown away! It seemed as if it had nothing to do with me. Then, in November, many things happened that opened a breach. First of all, I tested positive for Covid and so began isolation for twenty-five days in my

---

[8] As Daniélou points out, "This is the human drama of man today. Today we live in the universe of diffidence, in a world in which we have been subjected to so many deceptions that we no longer believe in the word true, and a world of this kind is frightening." J. Daniélou, *La cultura tradita dagli intellettuali* [Culture betrayed by intellectuals] (Milan: Rusconi, 1974), 28-29. Our translation from the Italian.

[9] "How can a person once grown old be born again? Surely he cannot reenter his mother's womb and be born again, can he?" (Jn. 3:4).

room. Paradoxically, this was a time when I felt the most accompanied by dear faces as well as new ones. During the month of isolation I was active in the organization of university elections and they were very intense days. The companionship I experienced during the month of November was something truly exceptional for me, even more so if I think of the particular circumstance in which everything happened. During the last days of quarantine there was also my birthday: while I was still in total isolation and far from friends and family, I had the opportunity to feel once again the enormous love and gratuitousness of all those special faces who in very creative ways accompanied me during the whole day. I feel truly grateful and fortunate. Azurmendi[10] met the Movement through the radio, and I was hooked again while I was alone in my room, through Zoom sessions and the elections. But did I have to be diagnosed with Covid to return to living things? Truly, there's nothing predictable and ordinary about the way the Mystery reaches us. So then I tell myself that the fundamental question is to ask to be open, which at times seems really difficult for me, and the more nothingness attacks my days, the more I struggle to do it."

It is already a big step forward to realize how fundamental this openness is. We often think that it is no big deal to remain open, but it is the fundamental

[10] Mikel Azurmendi, a Basque philosopher and anthropologist, has dealt in his long career with some of the most difficult themes of modern society, such as immigration, nationalism, jihad and the public value of the religious experience. He wrote about his encounter with Communion and Liberation in his book *El abrazo. Hacia una cultura del encuentro / L'Abbraccio. Verso una cultura dell'incontro*, published in Spain by Editorial Almuzara in 2018 and in Italy by Bur-Rizzoli in 2020. See here, p. 67.

question. Jesus said, "Blessed are the poor in spirit, for theirs is the kingdom of heaven."[11] In other words, that which can fulfill the expectancy of the heart must find openness in us, the willingness to let it enter, the "crack" through which its light can enter.[12]

I was saying that it seems impossible to us. But what if it happened? What if we encountered it? What if it came looking for us? What if, as Manuel Vilas wrote in *El Pais*, "the beauty of heaven fell upon all the men and women of this planet?"[13] If the unexpected happened, it would call for another moment of openness and sincerity, which is intimately connected with the exercise of reason and never in any way is a given. "The term 'reasonable' indicates those who submit their own reason to experience."[14] I will never tire of repeating this line by Jean Guitton, because it is so crucial for living. When something unexpected happens, you do verify, put to the test, your willingness to submit your reason to experience. This openness is a gesture of maturity that people reach only after a long journey, if they do not have the heart of a child.[15]

---

[11] Mt 5:3.

[12] Lewis wrote in this regard: "I cannot, by direct moral effort, give myself new motives. After the first few steps in the Christian life we realise that everything which really needs to be done in our souls can be done only by God. […] We, at most, allow it to be done to us." (C.S. Lewis, *Mere Christianity*, https://www.dacc.edu/assets/pdfs/PCM/merechristianitylewis.pdf, 41).

[13] M. Vilas, "La poesía", *El País*, December 29 2020. Our translation from the Italian translation.

[14] J. Guitton, *Arte nuova di pensare* [The New Art of Thinking] (Rome: Edizioni Paoline, 1981), 71. Our translation from the Italian translation.

[15] Lewis observed: "Christ never meant that we were to remain children in *intelligence*: on the contrary, He told us to be not only 'as harmless as doves,' but also 'as wise as serpents.' He wants a child's heart, but a grown-up's head." C.S. Lewis, *Mere Christianity*, 92.

Many situations can help us realize what kind of attitude we have. "I'm an operating room nurse but in November I was literally thrown into Covid intensive care. Given my desire to help people I thought I was up to it, but nothing could have been further from the truth! The reality I encountered was so hard that I couldn't bear it. Everything I was and thought I was, all the certainties were swept away when I crossed the threshold of that ward. I began to think I couldn't handle it and I asked to be transferred to another ward. But questions that wound you need an answer, not a change of circumstances, otherwise they remain there. So I returned to the Covid ward, and noticed first of all that there were very young colleagues who had been hired for the emergency, who were so passionate about their work and did it with such gusto that I was amazed and my own desire to be there was renewed. You need someone to follow whose face clearly expresses hope. You need someone who opens up the horizon again for you."

2. There are those who affirm that the unexpected has happened

"We've found the Messiah."[16] This news has travelled all through history: what our hearts awaited expectantly has made itself present. The unexpected of which Montale spoke has happened, in a place and in a time. This news has travelled through history since the day John and Andrew came upon Jesus of Naz-

16 Jn. 1:41.

areth on the shores of the Jordan River, a little more than two thousand years ago.

We who have been reached by this news find ourselves in front of the problem of its trustworthiness. Is Jesus of Nazareth truly who He says He is? Is He truly God made man? In fact, let's consider the content of the announcement. What supposedly happened? The unknown object of our expectancy, the infinite our heart yearns for, the "boundless" became a man, made Himself present. "The Word became flesh."[17]

Our calendars are still based on the date of that fact, that event. This is the year 2021 *after* the birth of Christ. But the pure verbal transmission of the news is not enough to make it believable for us; it is not sufficient for us to find it written in some religion or history book and every year on the calendar. How is its content to be verified? "How can those who encounter Jesus Christ a day, a month, a hundred, a thousand, or two thousand years [it is the same] after His disappearance from earthly horizons, be enabled to realize that he corresponds to the truth which He claims?"[18]

Let's begin by saying that since it happened in history as fact, it must be perceivable as fact today as well in order to be recognized as the fulfillment of our expectant awaiting. The original features of the Christian announcement must be respected. "One who is divine became man,"[19] a man you could meet on the

[17] Jn. 1:14.
[18] L. Giussani, *Why The Church*, trans. Viviane Hewitt (Montreal: McGill-Queen's University Press, 2001), 8.
[19] *Ibid.*, 18.

street, a fully human presence, that requires the method of an encounter.

Two thousand years ago, a fact fulfilled the infinite longing of women and men. Today discourses or rules, or reading the story in a book may be important but they cannot suffice for us. The human heart has not changed; the need for fullness has remained identical and only a fact can correspond to it. It is like the Covid vaccine: in order to verify its efficacy it must be something real, within everyone's reach. It is not enough to know it has been found; each person must be able to see and touch it, to discover its positive effects personally.

Thus, that "fact" of two thousand years ago must be something we can perceive today as it was for the first ones who encountered Jesus. But how can you and I, how can people today encounter this presence two thousand years later? What face, what features does it have? "Jesus Christ, that man of two thousand years ago, is concealed, becomes present, under the curtain, under the aspect of a different humanity. The encounter, the impact is with a different humanity: it is the experience of a different humanity that surprises us because it corresponds to the structural needs of the heart more than any modality of our thought or imagination. We did not expect it. We would never have dreamed it. It was impossible. It cannot be found elsewhere."[20]

This happened to Mikel Azurmendi, who, when he was gravely sick in the hospital, came upon something

---

[20] L. Giussani, *Un avvenimento nella vita dell'uomo* [An Event in the Life of Man] (Milan: Bur, 2020), 201. Our translation.

that transmitted a different humanity, a new accent compared to everything that had happened to him before. He heard a certain journalist on the radio who judged events differently than others, and Mikel recognized this as finally corresponding. When he left the hospital he met another person of the same group who looked at him in such a human way that it make Mikel experience an entirely unique correspondence to his elementary experience. Then he met another person, and another, and saw that all these people had the same accent, the same gaze; they were in reality in a different and more human way, and this attracted him, filling him with wonder and challenging him deeply.[21]

This dynamic can, or rather must happen also to those who have already had a certain encounter and live soaking in an experience like the Christian one, otherwise after the encounter you slide into the skepticism of Montale.

A young university student wrote me, "Until a few days ago it seemed that my life had lost its shine; I was beginning to wilt. One day my father received a call from work, saying that he needed to be tested for Covid as a precaution because he'd been in contact with an asymptomatic client. Two days later the result came back positive, and we all had to stay home in quarantine. The next week, after the danger had passed, I coasted on, as if just by inertia. I didn't even have the strength to call some friends because I was

---

[21] Cf. J. Carrón, *You only see what you admire*, Beginning Day for adults and university students of Communion and Liberation, online meeting, *clonline. org*, September 26, 2020.

convinced that in my home life there was no space for what you call an event. A few days later, fed up with this continuous floating, I tried with all my strength to throw myself into things like helping my mother with the house or cooking for the family, in order to regain some spurt or splash of true life, but it was no good, and the sense of limitation buried me even deeper. So I threw myself into studying. Time passed and I looked at the clock–it was 6:30 and I remembered that there was an online meeting of university students with you. I hesitated for a couple of minutes. Should I go? Should I skip it? Then I joined the meeting. At a certain point I heard someone say, 'After the experience of fullness during the university elections, which for that matter ended with an unexpected and very satisfying result, I sensed a strange malaise. How can I live that experience of fullness again, now that I've returned to my normal routine?' You began your answer by saying, 'The details that leave us with a strange malaise are crucial…' Something clicked up in me, and for the rest of the meeting I was glued to my computer waiting for other words that would restore my life to me. I left the Zoom meeting and returned to 'real life.' I had dinner, cleared the table, sat down to watch some television, and everything seemed normal, but when I went to bed I couldn't sleep. I kept thinking about what you said, and setting aside my pride, I prayed in such a human way that now when I look back, it still moves me. The next day, I was no longer myself! I have an 'absurd' serenity and this has mysteriously affected my interacting with the family, cooking and studying, with an unimaginable gladness. And just think, I didn't even want to join the meeting! I am overwhelmed with gratitude. What a wonder to live like this!"

We can recognize the truth of the announcement that reaches us today only by coming up against an event of human newness and experiencing the change that it generates in us, an "absurd" serenity (the adjective young people use today to say something is surprisingly great), an "unimaginable gladness," because you cannot give it to yourself. As Cabasilas wrote, it is a "new life, because it has nothing in common with the old one; it is better than you could even have imagined because even while it is of human nature, it is the life of God."[22]

3. The irreducible nature of the Christian fact

Let's take a better look at this "fact" that generates a new humanity. All of us are immersed in a history that transmits, for some a lot, for some not so much, the news of Christianity, provoking different reactions. Think once again of Azurmendi, a respected anthropologist and sociologist, who knew about Christianity, its doctrine, morality and values, but this knowledge was not what kindled his interest in Christianity when he was an older man. On the contrary, he had distanced himself years before and closed the door on it, as they say. Instead, what struck a spark in him a few years ago, such that he became curious and wanted to discover anew what Christianity is, knock-

[22] N. Cabasilas, *La vita in Cristo* [Life in Christ], 126.

ing down the wall built by his previous knowledge? What challenged his mindset, his stance? A "fact" that he could not explain as a scholar and as a man, that he could not fit into the categories with which he had looked at reality until then, including Christianity.

It was a "fact" that could not be subsumed or incorporated into his general outlook, something that could not be explained by the conceptual framework he used, by his usual thought patterns. The fact represented by that radio program, and then by the other encounters that happened after he left the hospital, could not be "subsumed," that is, led into and incorporated into one of Azurmendi's concepts or abstract universals, as Giussani said,[23] precisely because of the difference it contained. Its difference won him over. He was curious about and attracted by that fact and he became bound to it; he discovered he was glued to it. This introduced him to a new knowledge, a new way of treating everything, and it regenerated him. He became more himself. As the friend quoted before said, "The next day, I was no longer myself!" In other words, he was more herself.

Not everything can be pigeonholed into our habitual concepts, the frameworks into which we usually slot the things that happen. There are facts that cannot be reduced, that have something in them that challenges, breaks through, and exceeds the conceptual framework available. These "facts," we have often

[23] "The dominant mentality [...] when judging, always tends to subsume the particulars into an abstract universal." L. Giussani-S. Alberto-J. Prades, *Generating Traces in the History of the World*, trans. J. Patrick Stevenson (Montreal: McGill-Queen's University Press, 2010), 54.

said, are "*people, or moments of people*"[24] that carry within them a newness, a profoundly desirable human truth, without compare, that seems impossible. For this reason Saint Paul speaks of a "new creature." "Being a new man means being a person whose whole life announces, through what is already present in him, He who comes."[25] Those who come upon and let themselves be attracted by those facts, by those people, begin to experience the same newness in the way of living reality and are the first to discover "What a wonder to live like this!"

"Dear Julián, in the last six months, something has happened that has deeply marked my way of staying in front of everything. The nothingness of which we speak so much has entered my life brutally. On a day in June like any other, we received the news that my sister's boyfriend had unexpectedly killed himself. Those were days of great pain and upheaval. I stayed home with my sister to keep her company, but it was evident that no discourses, religious and not, could save us from the anguish this fact had evoked in us, opening a wound that bled constantly. Today, for me, what holds firm? What does it mean right now to say that Christ overcame death two thousand years ago? What does it mean to say that death is not the final word, above all in the case of someone who chooses it? How can life be more life? How can I live the hundredfold here below, now?" Everything she had been taught about the

---

[24] L. Giussani, *Easter Poster 1992*; the complete text in Italian is available in L. Giussani, *In cammino* [On the Way] *(1992-1998)* (Milan: Bur, 2014), 366.
[25] P. Evdokimov, *L'amore folle di Dio* [The mad love of God] (Cinisello Balsamo (Mi): San Paolo, 2015), 69. Our translation from the Italian translation.

promise of Christianity trembled in that earthquake. Is all this true? "And my sister? Is there hope? I had to acknowledge that right from the beginning, the companionship of certain friends slowly began to increase my awareness that Christ became flesh for me, so that I could experience the intimacy and concreteness of the relationship with Him. I experienced what you wrote in *The Radiance in Your Eyes*: "Christ is a contemporary presence, and recognition of this happens through the identical experience of two thousand years ago [...], namely, the impact with the presence of a different humanity that evokes a new presentiment of life. It strikes us because it corresponds like nothing else to our structural thirst for meaning and fullness. Then and now, it is the experience of an encounter that 'encompasses all meaning, value, desirableness, justness, beauty and pleasantness'." Christ was winning in me, in all my wounds and objections about those months, with His contemporary presence that passed through the human features of those friends in those days. His gaze generated in me the hope that nothing might be lost of that life apparently thrown away, of the intertwining of his life with my sister's and mine. I say so not because I'm obsessed or crazy but because this is my experience: for me it's impossible to separate the question 'Is there hope?' from His flesh present here and now."

The new creature is the fruit of this event. We see the vibration of the initial event now in the new subject it generates. Let's return once again to Giussani's words: the new creature has "a capacity for looking at and understanding reality that others cannot have." It is born "of the adherence to an event, from the affection for an event you have become attached to, that you have said *yes* to. This event is a particular detail in history. It has a universal claim, but it is a particular point. To take an event as a starting point for thought means first accepting that I am not the one who defines that event, but rather that the event defines me. What I really am and my conception of the world emerge in the event. This is a challenge for the dominant mentality, which, when judging, always tends to subsume the particulars into an abstract universal."[26]

The newness of the event also brings into life the verification, the demonstration of the truth of the initial encounter. In fact, how can I know whether the particular I run up against is the event of Christ today? I can know if it demonstrates, as in the testimonies just quoted, its "universal claim," its capacity to illuminate every circumstance or situation, even the most devastating: death.

"I am realizing with growing wonder that the origin of hope is the continual re-happening of an irreducible presence that corresponds totally to the heart. I realized that I have been given some facts that are supporting me and that I cannot reduce to someone's 'being nice' or their kindly temperament. In the beginning of December my very dear friend entered the monastic life. His full humanity, in love with life, his certainty of having encountered God and 'already having everything' because of this love–so much that he was able to leave everything because 'nothing is lost'–continue to be a point of no return for my days.

---

[26] L. Giussani-S. Alberto-J. Prades, *Generating Traces in the History of the World*, 53-54.

Simply by being in the monastery and with the very form of his life, he reminds me powerfully that the total answer to the expectant awaiting of my heart exists, and that I can encounter it. This is an enormous point of memory: I enter my days and things with a heart-thawing expectancy that makes me live a dialogue with everything. What is the connection between hope and his 'totally conquered' presence? A friend of mine discovered a few months ago that he has amyotrophic lateral sclerosis. In the midst of the drama of this circumstance, I cannot forget his face, which continually arrives in the evening and tells me, 'This evening, once again, I'm going to bed happy and grateful because of what I've seen and what has happened: the Lord is fulfilling His promise.' The illness continues to worsen and he is grateful. What sustains the possibility of total happiness of his heart, even in a situation in which there is absolutely nothing he can do? I don't see what he sees, but I see him, who is given to me. At the end of the year I asked some kids with whom I share the Scouting experience to join me for an evening on the first chapter of *The Religious Sense*, with the desire to give them the instrument that I'm discovering is of the most help for living: the heart. At the end of December I asked them to share the most beautiful thing that had happened during the year, and in a year of Covid, it was possible they'd only talk about difficulties, negativity and pain. But one of them said, 'Every time there's talk about the heart in a meeting or an encounter with someone, I wonder 'do I listen to my heart? Do I manage to follow it? It's the most precious discovery of this year!' I'm a teacher, and a few weeks ago when they closed the schools, in the initial frustration a question emerged in me: could it be that once again I'm being given an opportunity to learn to love those students who are here today and gone tomorrow? I went to Mass with this question and was moved to realize that even when we are under red zone Covid restrictions, even with school closed, Christ continues to give Himself to me. 'My heart is glad because You, Christ, live.' Here's the hope! Where do you live? In the impossible but real presence of my friend in the monastery, in the glad face of my friend who is going forward toward his destiny in his illness, in the Movement that generates me, allowing me to become aware of all this, to the point of betting on the heart of kids 'at the mercy of the waves' of the world. I'm seeing so many facts every day that make me experience the correspondence and remind me that Christ is alive and is everything! Only this sustains me. A few days ago, I brought a food package to a family as part of the charity work in which I participate. They offered me a coffee, and, full of all these facts, I decided for the first time to accept. The whole family was there in the living room, everybody properly distanced in respect of the Covid precautions. One of the daughters watched me in silence, and you could see she had a question inside: 'Why are you here? Why do you care about us?' When Christ dwells in your heart, all of reality, even a reality that is not yours, becomes a home you can inhabit. I thank the Movement on my knees for being the custodian of this humanly living gaze that is full of hope, because it is Him present, He who makes Himself flesh in my life."

In order to challenge the common mentality, the "fact" need not be anything clamorous. The power of the fact, of that particular detail, does not depend on its clamorous nature. It can be a mere breath of wind, but one that carries a difference that magnetizes you. Its power and uniqueness lie in the difference it bears. Azurmendi perceived it very well in the journalist he heard on the radio. In a 1980 dialogue with Giovanni Testori, Giussani indicated this fact by speaking of people who are "presences."[27]

We are often witnesses to facts like those described. However, it is not rare that instead of following them with simplicity like Azurmendi, we engulf them in our own system of thought, in the "already known," and therefore they do not tell us anything new. You can belong to the Christian story where many of these facts are seen, and yet continue to reduce Christianity to ethics or rites or stereotypes taken from the common image. However, none of these reductions can enkindle hope.

In the moment in which Christianity happens as an event and is embraced, we become aware of the difference that it introduces into life. Those who participate in Christianity as event unmask any reductive image of it. This happened to a young friend, who wrote, "A few days ago something happened that has helped me understand what has happened in my life. I was talking with my Mom about Christmas and at a certain point she said jokingly that she believes in Santa Claus because she needs to think there's a figure who brings hope, a face she can think of and say 'He can do every-

---

[27] "I find no other index of hope than the multiplication of these people who are presences. The multiplication of these people and an inevitable fondness [...] among these people." L. Giussani–G. Testori, *Il senso della nascita* [The Meaning of Birth] (Milan: Bur, 2013), 116.

thing; I'm placing my hope in him that everything will turn out ok.' Her comment made me understand the preference I have received in the Movement. My mother is a believer; she goes to Mass every Sunday, and yet she places her hope in Santa Claus because for her he is a definite, concrete face! It was a demonstration for me that at times God is reduced to something abstract, to an idea. Instead, I encounter God every day; He is present and I can recognize Him thanks to my being part of a history. Having discovered Him in the encounter with this particular story made hope spring up in me."

Running up against irreducible presences frees us from the condemnation of succumbing to the images taken from the common mentality. Only these presences bear within themselves, rooted in their innermost beings, the foundation of hope.

"The question 'Is there hope?' puts me with my back to the wall. I'm a medical student, and the healthcare situation makes the question all the more serious. In a period like this you can give theoretical answers to this question only for so long. At the end of the day, I lose sleep over these questions and they drain my strength. There must be a true answer that can stand up to the dramatic intensity of my days; a theoretical answer only makes everything harder to endure [it ends up increasing the nihilism, I would add]. Trying to answer the question 'Is there hope in front of my father's illness?' the only thing that enables me to answer is looking at him. Is there hope in front of the pandemic? The thing that comes to mind right away [it seems like a breath of wind] are the enthusiastic eyes of a friend who does not pull back in the midst of the exhausting work in the hospital. And so on. As I sift and weigh all the situations that are hard for me, the one thing that enables me to say there's some glimmer of hope is the example of people for whom this hope exists. However, here the drama intensifies and is not placated. Seeing them, I feel a great desire to be like them and be able to stay in front of life with their same eyes [as happened to Azurmendi, who said to himself, 'How I would like to look at the world the way this journalist does!'], but I realize that it can't be my own effort, otherwise at the end of the day I'd just go to bed tired of counting every success or failure [it would be like reducing everything again to ethics]. So I ask myself, 'what's the use?' Every day I'm surprised by someone who lives with truth, who attracts me and sets me into motion because I envy their way of looking at the same identical things that I'm already fed up with by eight in the morning. Usually this attraction fades two hours later, but sometimes it makes me really get engaged myself. So I ask myself whether it is sufficient to follow them. Is it enough to stay in relationship with these real presences who like stars mark my days and, even if for just a moment, make me feel understood, with all my difficulties and crises?"

The answer to this question poses a problem of freedom. In front of presences who bear within them the foundation of hope, each person must first of all decide whether to follow the desire to be like them and be in their company, or not.

4. Experience and the criteria of the heart

How can you recognize these presences for what they are, for what they bear, for their true value, all the way to the origin of their difference? This question concerns us, and not even the apostles were spared it. In fact, they were the first ones who had to face it.

When the presence of Jesus began to impose itself and His fame started spreading because of the things He said and did, different interpretations about Him also began to circulate, with the complicity of those who felt their power and "authority" undermined, that is, the Pharisees and scribes, the intellectuals and leaders of the people. How did the first people who took up with Him understand that it was worthwhile to follow Him, to bind themselves to Him, to wager all their life on Him?

How do you recognize among the many faces, *the* face? What criterion can be used? By now, it should be familiar to us; we should have learned it from experience. The one adequate criterion for recognizing the presences that bring an adequate meaning to life is the one with which nature projects us in the universal comparison with everything we encounter: the heart, namely, that set of needs–for truth, beauty, justice, and happiness–and evidence that emerge in us when we are engaged with what we pass through. Giussani said, "In experience, the reality [...] by which [...] you are struck, shocked (*affectus*), causes the criteria of the heart to leap up; it awakens the heart that previously was confused and sleeping, therefore it awakens you to yourself. This is where your journey begins, because you are awake and critical."[28]

---

[28] L. Giussani, *Si può (veramente?!) vivere così?* [Is it (really?!) possible to live this way?] (Milan: Bur, 2011), 83. Our translation.

These criteria that operate inside us even in spite of ourselves are objective and infallible, and they do not spare us one bit. Pavese documented this dramatically. On July 14, 1950, after he received the Strega Prize [the most prestigious Italian literary award], he wrote "Came from Rome, some time ago. At Rome, apotheoses. But now, this is it."[29] It was as if the thing he himself noted in his diary years before had come true. "There is something even sadder than failing short of one's own ideals: to have realized them."[30] Less than a year before his death he confessed, "How many times in these last entries have you written *And then*? Aren't you getting into a rut?"[31] In fact, on June 22, 1950, when he received news of the great success, he wrote "It is a great stroke of good fortune, no doubt, but how many times will it still bring me pleasure? And then?"[32] What was missing from his life, which seemed so successful in the eyes of the world? On August 17, 1950 he wrote, "Names do not matter. They are only names that chanced to drift my way; if not those, there would have been others. What remains is that now I know what will be my greatest triumph–and this triumph lacks flesh and blood, life itself."[33] Under the weight of that lack, ten days later he committed suicide!

[29] C. Pavese, "14th July 1950,", in Id., *This Business of Living: Diaries 1935-1950*, 348.

[30] C. Pavese, "18th December 1937," in *Ibid.*, 64.

[31] C. Pavese, "16th October 1949," in *Ibid.*, 328.

[32] C. Pavese, "22nd June 1950," in *Ibid.*, 348.

[33] C. Pavese, "17th August 1950," in *Ibid.*, 350.

Camus noted a similar experience in his *Notebooks* on the day of his great success. "*October 17.* Nobel. Strange sensation of despondency and melancholy."[34]

We cannot elude the constitutive criteria of the heart, the need for meaning, justice, happiness, and love. They can be silenced or censured up to a certain point, but they cannot be uprooted. They are internal to experience. Giussani denounced our difficulty in recognizing that "the principle of judgment of experience lies in experience itself." But, he stressed, "if it were not true that the principles with which to judge one's own experience lie within experience itself, people would be alienated because they would have to depend on something other than themselves to judge themselves."[35] These needs are not born in what people experience, but "are born in them in front of what they experience, in them engaged in what they go through,"[36] and these needs judge what they experience.

The criterion for judging must "emerge from within the inherent structure of the human being, the structure at the origin of the person." This "fundamental criterion for facing things is an objective one, with which nature thrusts man into a universal comparison, endowing him with that nucleus of original needs, with that elementary experience which mothers in the *same* way provide to their children. It is only here, by affirming this

[34] A. Camus, *Taccuini. 1951-1959 [Notebooks.]*, III (Milan: Bompiani, 1992), 223. Our translation from the Italian translation.
[35] L. Giussani, *Si può (veramente?!) vivere così?* [Is it (truly?!) possible to live this eay?], 83-84.
[36] *Ibid.*, 82.

common identity, that we overcome anarchy,"[37] subjectivism.

You cannot speak of experience simply in terms of 'going through' something. "The category of *experience* as we use the word has an absolutely critical value," Giussani said. It should not be understood as "sentimental immediacy," but as "the place where the impact with reality provokes the constitutive needs of the human heart, developing the search for an answer to the provocations of reality." Consequently, "*Experience* is therefore the sphere in which the person is called to verify whether the fact of Christ–the true, great working hypothesis–can respond to these questions with a vision of the factors marked by an authenticity and completeness that none of the other proposals have." He quickly added, "Therefore, the main intent of CL is its desire to rediscover and live authentically the fact that the Christian faith, as it has been maintained in the mainstream of orthodoxy, responds better than any other proposal to the deep needs of the human person."[38]

This is why the true disaster of today is the weakening of the consciousness of these needs, the obscuring of the awareness of one's identity. In fact, Christ came to respond to human beings, not to "arid beings like robots." As Reinhold Niebuhr wrote, and I quoted before, "Nothing is more unbelievable than the answer

---

[37] L. Giussani, *The Religious Sense*, 7, 10.

[38] L. Giussani, "Il ragionevole ossequio della fede [The reasonable respect for faith]," interview by A. Metalli, *30Giorni*, n. 5, 1988, pp. 40-41. Our translation.

to a question that is not asked." Thus here is "the main intent of CL": to "testify to the reasonableness of the faith, faith as *reasonable respect*, reasonable defined according to the conception of Saint Thomas–the experience of a correspondence between the proposal of faith and the structural needs of the human consciousness."[39]

The Christian event is different because of the experience it generates. The fact of the encounter with Jesus provoked in the disciples the experience of an incomparable correspondence. "We have found the Messiah." All the other favorable events, which of course we wish will happen in life, including the successes we manage to achieve, do not satisfy the expectant awaiting or keep the promise, and in the end are a source of deep disappointment. In front of them, we too share Pavese's reaction: "And now?".

Let's return to the point. Authentic experience, as the place of knowledge and verification, cannot be identified as a simple subjective impression or a sentimental reaction. Experience is a "single, vital act and it is composed of three elements: a) An *encounter* with an objective fact originally independent from the person having the experience. [...] b) The power to adequately perceive the meaning of this encounter. [...] c) An *awareness of the correspondence* between the meaning of the Fact we have come across and the meaning of our own existence [...]. It is our awareness of this correspondence that verifies the growth of self that is essential to the phenomenon of experi-

---

[39] *Ivi.*

ence." Therefore, in an authentic experience "human self-awareness and critical thinking"[40] are engaged.

This is what the prophet Isaiah said in another way. "That You would rend the heavens and come down!" or in other words, that the unexpected would happen, that God would truly respond to our expectant awaiting, "with the mountains quaking before You."[41] The sign that the promise has been fulfilled is the leap of your heart, the repercussion provoked by the event. This is what happened to Elizabeth. "When Elizabeth heard Mary's greeting, the infant leaped in her womb."[42] It is the same leap of the heart felt by John and Andrew when, after they came upon Jesus and spent the afternoon with Him, they told everyone "We have met the Messiah!" This is the leap of the heart also felt by Azurmendi. "I never expected to encounter any of all this in my life. It was a great surprise. Entirely out of the usual [...]; little by little, I entered into an emotional state of wonder."[43] The leap of the heart is the sign that this event is happening again.

Therefore, I can recognize the divine present in certain presences, as Elizabeth recognized Jesus in Mary's womb, through the correspondence to my heart, to my humanity, that I experience in the encounter with them and that manifests itself in the "leap of the heart." And the verification of this encounter is its capacity to

[40] L. Giussani, *The Risk of Education*, trans. Mariangela Sullivan, (Montreal: McGill-Queen's University Press, 2019), 87.

[41] Is 63:19.

[42] Lk 1:41.

[43] "L'abbraccio [The Embrace]," transcript of the television interview with Mikel Azurmendi, done by Fernando de Haro for the Meeting 2020, in J. Carrón, *You only see what you admire*, 15.

introduce me to the totality of reality, to make me face every situation and to challenge any circumstance. "Christ brought all newness by bringing Himself,"[44] said Saint Irenaeus. He brought the newness of each thing. What experience must the first Christians have had to describe Christ in such a way!

It happened and it continues to happen. It happened a few months ago to the barista of a café near the university, whose patrons were prevalently students.

"We CLU members are among the few students who continue going to the university to use the few study rooms that are open. Every morning we get a coffee (carry-out) from the same café and we've become friends with the barista. Last Friday morning my cousin was the last to enter and he asked the man, who has worked in that bar since 1982, how things were going. He replied, 'Look, there's not much work, but fortunately there are you guys. I know you're in CL. You can see it a mile away, because you're like those of thirty years ago: you're the only ones who bring a breath of fresh air to the university zone.' I wondered how it was possible for him to recognize that we were in CL and say that it's the same thing as thirty years ago. Above all, how is it possible that we, including me, are defined as the only ones who bring a breath of fresh air to the university zone? The reason doesn't lie in some ability of mine or ours. No, the issue is that I've had an encounter that scratched and marked my heart permanently to the point of making my way of looking at reality different from everyone else's. So there's

---

[44] "*Omnem novitatem attulit, semetipsum afferens.*" Saint Irenaeus, *Adversus Haereses*, IV, c. 34, n. 1. *Adversus haereses*, IV, c. 34, n.1: PG 7 pars prior, 1083.

no need for me to do astonishing things. I just have to be myself. Therefore I've grown in the awareness that in the end, either Christ exists or there is *nada*, nothing! It's this way because in my experience so many facts have happened that they've become like successive "coats of glue" that made and make me stick to this companionship, so much so that I say "Far from You, where do I go?" I live in this time, and in front of the facts of the situation I'm not desperate, because of the experience I have. It's an expansion of my faith to the future, as well. The weapon for waging my daily battle against the challenge of this situation is trust, faith. Having this certainty, without doing anything in particular, but just being myself, I bring something more than just me. Now, I live the present with hope."

For the barista it was easy to recognize the difference in those young people, because of the breath of fresh air they brought to his life.

CHAPTER 4

THE FLOWER OF HOPE

Now we have to face this truly thorny problem, the most sensitive point for all of us, children as we are of so-called Western culture.

1. A need for certainty

How can we, who live in this time and in this culture–I think above all of young people, who are familiar with the calculating rationality of science and technology and are structurally intolerant of everything that is not immediate and measurable, and comes off as doctrine–reach certainty about Christ? Today this need is particularly felt. Anyone who deals with young people knows this well. Giussani grasped it early and this need has grown even stronger today, when there is no longer any inertia driving Christian faith. Lucio Brunelli wrote of this recently in *L'Osservatore Romano*, speaking of today's youth. "Christ, dead and risen, salvation of the human person. You can yell this truth in his face […] but that young man will look at you perhaps […] with indifference," as if looking at something "incomprehensible."[1] Christian faith is no lon-

---

[1] L. Brunelli, "Le chiese vuote e la fantasia di Dio [The empty churches and the imagination of God]," *L'Osservatore Romano*, April 10, 2021, p. 9.

ger a social fact, an obvious premise; it is not part of our education, and therefore we are "forced" to rediscover how it arrives, which to my mind is a fortunate thing, as in a certain sense now we are obliged to have a reasonable and well-founded faith.

Let's ask ourselves: what was the foundation of the faith of the first ones who followed Jesus? The same thing holds for us today. From the very beginning of his educational work, Giussani was acutely aware of the urgent need for the reasonableness of faith. This is another way the grace of the charism, and the pertinence to our needs as people today (immersed as we are in an uncertainty we do not know how to overcome) of the grace given to Fr. Giussani, make themselves evident. The reality born of this grace has one goal, as said in the quotation given before: to testify to the reasonableness of the faith, that is, that the fact of Christ responds better than any other proposal to the deep needs of our humanity. In fact, it is reasonable to believe and belong because the event of Christ corresponds to the structural needs of human consciousness. And "the proposal to young people is a very clear test"[2] of the awareness or lack thereof of this urgent need for reasonableness.

What is needed so that young people and adults can discover the reasonableness of faith? At the Synod on the Laity in 1987, Giussani spoke of the situation of contemporary people. "Endowed with operative possibilities like never before in history, they struggle greatly to perceive Christ as the clear and certain

---

[2] L. Giussani, "Il ragionevole ossequio della fede [The Reasonable Respect for Faith]," interview by A. Metalli, *30Giorni*, p. 40.

response to the meaning of their own ingeniousness." He said that institutions often fail to offer this response in a vital way. "What is missing is not so much the verbal or cultural repetition of the announcement. People today are waiting, perhaps unconsciously, for the experience of encounter with people for whom the fact of Christ is a reality so present that their life is changed. Human impact is what can jolt people today–an event that reechoes as initial event, when Jesus raised His eyes and said, 'Zacchaeus, come down here, I'm coming to your house'."[3]

The point of departure is the experience of an encounter, just as it was two thousand years ago. It cannot be any other way now, because it would not be Christianity. "It is the great inversion of method that marks the passage from the religious sense to faith: it is no longer a search full of unknowns, but the discovery of a fact that happened in the history of women and men." The testimonies I quoted document this. "This is the condition without which you cannot even speak about Jesus Christ. Instead, Christ becomes familiar along this road, almost the way the relationship with your own mother and father over time becomes increasingly constitutive of who you are." From the experience of the encounter with His humanity, which has the face, the aspect of concrete people, of a certain

[3] L. Giussani, from *L'avvenimento cristiano. Uomo Chiesa Mondo* (Milan: Bur, 2003), 23-24. English translation from the description of the Synod speech *Lay, That is Christian* in *Life of Fr. Giussani*, Alberto Savorana, trans. Mariangela C. Sullivan and Christopher Bacich (Montreal: McGill-Queen's University Press, 2018), 753-754.

companionship, we are led by an experienced correspondence to the "great question about His divinity."[4]

The urgent need for the reasonableness of faith regards people of all ages–both young and adults–and conditions of life.

The words of a university student are meaningful and emblematic of the problem. "The question of certainty about Christ is an open one for me. After many years in the Movement, the moment of Mass and Communion are deeply uncomfortable for me because I don't believe any more. I'm grateful to my friends in the Movement for the intensity of life that cyclically returns to reclaim me, but I can't ignore the fact that the Movement is based on the 'incredible' fact of Christ, incredible for me, and I can't manage to accept it. I ask, how can Christ be there, how can He be in me? I don't understand where Christ is, in whom, if we are all limited human beings. I don't feel this is skepticism: I believe that finally I'm not hiding the fact that certain things don't convince me and I can't pretend they do. It's like I'm in front of a bicycle wheel, and I see all the spokes, the human spokes, all the things that have happened to me, the people, but I can't see the center of these spokes; it seems forced, an autosuggestion. I see that the love I experience comes from my mother and father, my friends, at times more and at times less, and I don't understand well how at a certain point Christ comes into play."

[4] L. Giussani, *All'origine della pretesa Cristiana* [At the Origin of the Christian Claim] (Milan: Rizzoli, 2011), VI. The English translation contains a shorter version of this text. The translation here is ours.

I am grateful to this friend for the boldness and bluntness of her request, first of all, because it is the sign she finds herself in a companionship in which she feels free to ask radical questions. And as each of you can acknowledge, it is not always the case that there is a place where a person can ask her questions, expose her doubts, and risk without fear.

Before responding to her question, I'd like to propose another testimony that moves from the same perspective.

"These are very hard times: many people are sick with Covid and many suffer from 'ordinary' illnesses that often are not treated well because the healthcare system is not receptive according to its normal regulations. Then there are the economic difficulties that are becoming grave for many people. The fear of living and dying gnaws at the flesh and heart even of those who apparently have no significant problems. There is a kind of existential 'suspension' that causes anxiety and even anguish. In this situation, more than before, it's inevitable to ask yourself what's truly essential. In our School of Community we've been asking ourselves about this a lot, and everyone believes that in addition, naturally, to personal relationships and work, the community to which we belong is essential for us. But among some of us, there are doubts about what this really means. We live the community carnally every day, not just in the moment of School of Community. It's our home, our source of council, comfort, and support, often in concrete ways. It's the place of fraternal love that we touch. I would say that the big difficulty is with God. Some of us have no doubts about their relationship with Him, but others feel a heart-thawing need, an endless longing. For them, faith isn't simply trusting and entrusting themselves to Him, but a search. We become seekers of God, like the ancient people of Israel, and we're afraid. What if it's only an illusion that we've built for ourselves, without any foundation? This is our great fear! Nobody has ever seen God, but His signs can be seen after the coming of His Son, and this should be enough for us. But how can I comfort not only myself in the darkness of daily fear, but also friends who are already suffering concretely in the flesh? How can I tell them about God? How can I find the peace that enables me to face every circumstance, even the most negative, with serenity and trust? How can I have trust in salvation, just looking at the people surrounding me, without seeing and touching Him? Without God each thing loses meaning, and this is indisputable. How can the desire for faith become a faith truly lived?"

These testimonies express a cry. They are not skeptics, but young people and adults who do not settle for suppressing their impatience with just any answer. We see Dostoyevsky's question throbbing in them: "Can a cultured man, a European of our days, believe, really believe in the divinity of the Son of God, Jesus Christ?"[5] Like every genius, Dostoyevsky was prophetic, noting ahead of his time what would become everyone's urgent question.

These "seekers" are looking for a road to travel to reach reasonable certainty about what they have encountered.

---

[5] Cf. F.M. Dostoevskij, *I demoni; Taccuini per "I demoni"* [The Demons, Notebooks for "The Demons"], edited by E. Lo Gatto (Florence: Sansoni, 1958), 1011.

Without this certainty, the desired hope will not find an adequate foundation and it will be impossible for freedom to adhere, to the point of affection, to the very reality they have come across. Clearly, the problem of hope requires attention to the certainty of faith.

In the light of this existential need, we can better appreciate the method Giussani showed us; we can realize its value and not shelve it among the boxes of things we already know, in the name of a certain familiarity with the concepts. By following this method, we can verify whether the road he shows leads each of us from "desire for faith" to "a truly lived faith."

a) The method of moral certainty

Each of us in our own way feels the need to reach certainty about Christ in order to stay in front of our own needs for fullness, truth, and justice, and in front of the problems with which life never ceases to tax us. So then, let's focus on the request in the testimonies: how can we know and recognize Christ with certainty? As we have said, it is the question of faith. Now, faith is one of reason's ways of knowing, not mere easy sentimentalism. It is the knowledge of something I do not see, through the mediation of an other. I do not see the object directly, immediately, but I come to know about it through a witness. "Culture, history, and society are based on this type of knowledge called faith, […] knowledge of reality through the mediation of a witness." Here we are interested in developing the question of faith on a particular level, "the most important level of all the important levels of life, the greatest level of life. It's the level that has to do with destiny."[6]

Giussani continued his line of reasoning. "We don't know Christ directly. We know Chrst neither through evidence nor through the analysis of experience," just as two thousand years ago John and Andrew did not directly see the divine in that man they had come across, Jesus of Nazareth. We are in the same situation. Since Christ is the total object of our faith, the question arises, "How do we come to know Christ in such a way that the sacrifice of our entire lives can be upheld by Him?"[7] If faith is that form of knowledge based on the mediation of a witness, the first problem concerns reaching certainty about the trustworthiness of the witness.

What road must we travel in order to reach certainty about a person? Among the different methods by which reason can reach certainty in the various spheres of reality, the one that interests us here is the method regarding human behavior. In fact, one method leads to mathematical certainties, another to scientific certainties, yet another to philosophical certainties, but there is a fourth method of reason that leads to certainties about human behavior, moral certainties. In some way, it "is closer to the approach of the artist or genius," who reach the intuition of truth starting from signs. "When Newton saw the famous apple fall, it became a *sign* that immediately produced his great hypothesis. Genius needs only a small indication to reach a universal intuition. The method by which I understand that my

[6] L. Giussani, *Is It Possible to Live This Way?*, Vol. 1, *Faith*, trans. John Zucchi (Montreal: McGill-Queen's University Press, 2008), 9-10.
[7] *Ibid.*, 25.

mother loves me and through which I am certain that many people are my frends cannot be fixed mechanically; my intelligence intuits that the only reasonable meaning, the only reasonable inerprtation of the convergence of a given set of 'signs' is this. If these signs, in their hundreds and thousands, could be indefinitely multiplied, their only adequate meaning would be that my mother loves me."[8]

On many occasions I have used the example of a mother to demonstrate the method by which you reach certainty about another person: the reading of the signs. If someone were to ask me, "How can I see that my mother loves me?" I would say, "You can see it from the signs. Not everyone does what your mother does for you."[9] Having seen many signs, being honest about what you have seen, you will be able to recognize that everything your mother does has only one explanation, only one point of convergence, like the bicycle spokes our friend described, and it is called love. You can call it X instead of love, but nonetheless your mother's behavior is full of signs of unconditional affirmation of your being that makes you certain of her and enables you to trust her. Love is not something that scientific instruments can ever certify through analyses or experiments: love is the meaning of the signs.

---

[8] L. Giussani, *The Religious Sense*, 19-20.

[9] Von Balthasar observed, "In those who ask questions, it is useful to awaken the elementary sense for mystery and its respect. Since most human beings have loved at least once, they can be reminded of certain laws and experiences of love and led from here toward the love of God." H.U. von Balthasar, *Il chicco di grano. Aforismi* [The grain of wheat. Aphorisms] (Milan: Jaca Book, 1994), 42. Our translation.

Giussani continued, "The demonstration of a moral certainty is the consequence of a complex of indications whose only adequate meaning–whose only adequate motive and whose only reasonable reading–is that certainty itself." It can be called not only "a moral certainty, but also an *existential certainty*," inasmuch as "it is bound to the moment at which you examine the phenomenon, that is, when you intuit all of the signs. An example: I am not worried that the person now in front of me may want to kill me; not even after this statement does this person want to kill me, if only for the satisfaction of proving that I am wrong. I reach this conclusion by reading certain facets of his behaviour and a specific situation. But I could not be as certain about the future, when the circumstances might be different."[10]

At this point, Giussani looked at two important points.

In the first place, I "will be able to be certain about you, to the extent that I pay more attention to your life, that is, that I share in your life. The signs leading to certainty become multiplied in the measure in which you pay attention to them. For example, in the Gospel, who was able to understand the need to trust that man? Not the crowd looking for a cure, but those who followed Him and shared His life. Life together (*convivenza*) and shared!".[11] If I stand there watching, and say, "Beautiful!" but then leave, I lose everything. If I do not follow the repercussion, the leap of the heart that a certain presence provokes in me, I lose it, I lose the best of what has happened to me. If you see a person once and then you never see that person again, the perception of truth you in fact had can fade. We

[10] L. Giussani, *The Religious Sense*, p. 20.
[11] *Ivi*.

want to understand in a hurry, before committing ourselves, without getting involved. But how can you reach
certainty without getting involved? It would be make-be-
lieve. Instead, when you get involved and follow the repercussion you felt, the signs multiply and your conviction
deepens. And since experience does not deceive us, if we
have made a mistake we realize it very soon. "Ah no, this
wasn't what I intuited."[12]

Secondly, and inversely, Giussani stressed, "the more
powerfully one is human, the more one is able to become certain about another on the basis of only a few
indications. This is the human genius, the genius that
is able to read the truth of behaviour, of man's way of
life. The more powerfully human one is, the more one is
able to perceive with certainty. 'To trust is good, but not
to trust is better.' This proverb offers a rather superficial
kind of wisdom because the capacity to trust another is
proper to the strong and secure man. The insecure man
does not even trust his own mother. The more one is
truly human, the more one is able to trust, because one
understands the reasons for believing in another."[13]

b) A very human trajectory

As we said, in order to know a person, shared life is
needed, and this takes time. Only those willing to

---

[12] The "solutions [here] are reached not so much through lines of reasoning,
as through reason, with the truth itself of things and with experience" (William of Saint-Thierry, [*On the Nature and Dignity of Love*, 31]. Our translation from the Italian translation "Natura e valore dell'amore," 31, in Id.,
Opere/3 (Rome: Città Nuova, 1998), 97.
[13] L. Giussani, *The Religious Sense*, 20.

invest the time required will attain adequate and reasonably grounded certainty about the person. This shared living over time evidently demands attention to the signs that the person offers about herself. It is a very human trajectory with an unmistakable starting point. "When we meet a person who is to be significant in our lives, there is always that first instant when we have a presentiment, when something inside us is almost forced by the evidence of an unavoidable recognition: 'That's him' or 'That's her'."[14]

In a certain sense the beginning already contains everything, as conveyed in the expression "evidence of an unavoidable recognition." The unavoidable character of the recognition may cause you to think that the journey is already over, that you have already reached definitive knowledge, but this is not the case, as the experience of each of us can confirm. If you want to reach certainty about the other person, that evidence is the beginning of a journey that must be made. Therefore, Giussani continued, "But only space and time dedicated to reiterating this evidence will bolster the existential weight of our initial impression. Only sharing life (*convivenza*) enables this impression to penetrate ever more radically and deeply within us until, at a certain point, it is absolute."[15]

It is the same issue, whether you encounter an important person in the broad sense, or whether you encounter Christ, the Christian companionship. For John and Andrew, for Peter and the others, it was necessary to travel this progressive journey of knowledge,

[14] L. Giussani, *At the Origin of the Christian Claim*, 50.
[15] *Ivi.*

made up of repetitions, signs that accumulated, as it is for us. "And this road of 'knowing' will be confirmed over and over again in the Gospel, that is, it will need reinforcement, for the formula 'and His disciples believed in Him,' is repeated many times, until the end." We cannot avoid it, and it is not to our advantage to do so. "This knowing will be a slow process of persuasion and no subsequent step will negate the prior ones–even at the beginning they had believed. From sharing His life would emerge a confirmation of that exceptional, different quality that had struck them from the first moment. In sharing His life that confirmation grows."[16]

The distance between the first perception or impression charged with evidence, and certainty, involves the trajectory of the "conviction through a series of repeated recognitions which must be given space and time." It is a law that brooks no exceptions. "If it is true that knowledge of an object requires time and space, there is all the more reason for this law to apply to an object claiming to be unique. Even those first to encounter this uniqueness had to follow this same road."[17] For us, as well, this road is necessary. Each of us can decide whether to travel it or to give up. Everything depends on the willingness with which, following the correspondence, the repercussion, the initial leap of the heart in the encounter, we verify its import, without forcing things, giving ourselves the time needed to attain certainty.

[16] *Ibid.*, 51.
[17] *Ibid.*, 51.

c) An incomparable presence

The same thing happens in a relationship of affection. How long does a child need to share life with his mother to reach certainty that she loves him and he can trust her? Normally we do not take this process into consideration, only because it unfolds imperceptibly. The same thing happens in shared life with Christ, with the human reality of His presence today: we are overwhelmed every day not only by gestures and signs similar to those a mother can give, but also by signs that bear within a difference from those any mother naturally can offer.

Let's read from Mark's Gospel. "When Jesus returned to Capernaum after some days, it became known that He was at home. Many gathered together so that there was no longer room for them, not even around the door, and He preached the word to them. They came bringing to Him a paralytic carried by four men. Unable to get near Jesus because of the crowd, they opened up the roof above Him. After they had broken through, they let down the mat on which the paralytic was lying. When Jesus saw their faith, He said to the paralytic, 'Child, your sins are forgiven.' Now some of the scribes were sitting there asking themselves, 'Why does this man speak that way? He is blaspheming. Who but God alone can forgive sins?' Jesus immediately knew in His mind what they were thinking to themselves, so He said, 'Why are you thinking such things in your hearts? Which is easier, to say to the paralytic, Your sins are forgiven, or to say, Rise, pick up your mat and walk? But that you may know that the Son of Man has authority to forgive sins on earth'–He said to the paralytic, 'I say to you, rise, pick up your mat, and go home.' He rose, picked up his mat at once, and went away in the sight of everyone. They were all astounded and glorified God, saying, 'We have never seen anything like this'."[18]

The healing of the paralytic left all those present speechless. "They were all astounded." But the import of this sense of wonder grew with His "claim" to forgive sins. "'But that you may know that the Son of Man has authority to forgive sins on earth'–He said to the paralytic, 'I say to you, rise, pick up your mat, and go home'." Jesus leads us to the recognition of one thing through the other one. This opened a breach in those who witnessed it. "They were all astounded and glorified God." What they saw was a sign that pointed to God, who aced through the exceptional nature of the presence they had in front of them and that caused them to exclaim "We have never seen anything like this!" Now let's put ourselves in the shoes of Peter, Andrew, John and the others who, spending every day with Jesus, saw Him heal the paralytic, give sight to the man born blind, and calm the storm while they were in the boat. Not only. He had a gaze on them, other people, and all of reality that was different from that of any other person: it was incomparably human. They found themselves in front of signs that were as concrete and irreducible as those of a mother, but at the same time, incomparable, signs of the exceptional nature of a presence that corresponded to their heart like nothing else. They too, like the others, more than the others, said "We have never seen anything like this!"

18 Mk 2:1-12.

There was a moment in the journey of the disciples when the certainty they had reached about His person, the awareness of His uniqueness became explicit. Let's follow the way Giussani made us relive that moment.

That day Jesus was followed by a huge crowd that "forgot to eat, didn't feel tired, even though it had been almost three days since they followed Him, so they could hear Him speak." Coming to the crest of the hill, Jesus "saw this sea of people covering the sides of the hill 'and had pity on them'. [...] So He told the apostles: 'Have them all sit down'." They sat down and He fed them all. In front of this most recent gesture, many of those who had been following Him to hear Him speak were seized by an irresistible fascination, "a roar of praise swelled up, and they all began to shout to Christ as the king who was to come." The next day was the Sabbath and He went, as was His custom, to the synagogue. That Sabbath "the Bible passage was the story of the Hebrews in the desert, whom God fed with the manna. And Jesus said: 'Your fathers ate manna in the desert, but they died. I will give you manna, I will give you a bread such that whoever eats it will no longer die.' [...] 'I will give you My flesh to eat and My blood to drink. And whoever eats this bread and drinks this blood will live forever'." Upon hearing these words, the reaction of those present, first among them the scribes and pharisees, exploded violently. "'Did you hear? He's crazy, crazy! Who can give his own flesh to eat, his own blood to drink? He's crazy, crazy!' [...] Slowly, the people followed the Pharisees and scribes and everyone left the synagogue." But a small group remained. The twelve remained there in silence. Jesus looked at them and asked "'And you too, do you want to go away?' He doesn't mitigate the inconceivability of what He said, but insists: 'And you too, do you want to go away?' As usual, Simon impetuously made himself everyone's spokesman and said: 'Master, we don't understand what you say either, but if we go away from you, where shall we go? Only you have the words'–the real translation should be–'that correspond to the heart, that give meaning to life.' But what does 'words that correspond to the heart' mean? Reasonable words! Reason is to understand the correspondence […] 'I don't understand this, but if I go away from Him no one will speak to me according to my heart'."[19]

Thus their immediate reaction was expressed by Peter. "'We must follow you because you're the only person, the only case that's so exceptional, where a person speaks in a way that always corresponds to the heart. And if now you tell us something different, it means that we don't understand it, for now. You'll explain it to us. We'll understand it tomorrow, but we can't leave you just because we don't understand these words.' […] And, in fact, whoever went away contradicted themselves, went away contradicting themselves." What is the most reasonable position? "The right thing to have done is what Peter and his other friends did: they followed Him just the same. 'We may not understand, nevertheless no one speaks according to the human heart as you do, so if we go away from You where shall we go? Life would have no more meaning'." This, Giussani stresses, is "the beginning of an affective attitude. The others went away refusing Him, regardless of what they had seen and heard. This little group remained, adhering to Him, following Him. It's the beginning of the concept of obedience that

[19] L. Giussani, *Is It Possible to Live This Way?*, Vol. 1, *Faith*, 118-123.

is born […] as a reasonable attitude. […] It was right to follow Him, since otherwise they would have had to negate all the preceding months when they were with Him, in which it became clear to them that that man was a man different from the rest."[20]

Here we see clearly the journey that bound the disciples to Him more and more. Every day they were more "seized." Jesus became the focus of their affections. "Man's life consists in the affection that chiefly sustains him and in which he finds the greatest satisfaction."[21] We are called to make the same crucial journey. In these years I have often recalled what Giussani told me in a certain circumstance. "Look, Julián, in the end, the difference is between those who have done a stable work and those who have not."

d) Faith is the recognition of a Presence

The more the signs of His exceptional nature multiplied, the more they felt a paradoxical question explode in them, because they knew everything that could be known about Him, a question they were unable to answer but it was necessary to answer: "Who is this man?".[22] It was provoked by the continual wonder at the exceptional nature of His presence. In fact, in their experience of shared living with Jesus, a factor of the reality of that man emerged more and more, and no matter how often they tried, they could

[20] *Ibid.*, 123-126.
[21] Saint Thomas Aquinas, *Summa Theologiae*, II, II^{ae}, q. 179, a. 1.
[22] Cf. Mt 8:27.

not explain it, but at the same time, they could not eliminate it.

At a certain point, when they were in the environs of Caesarea Philippi, "He asked His disciples, 'Who do people say that the Son of Man is?' They replied, 'Some say, John the Baptist, others Elijah, still others, Jeremiah or one of the prophets'." Jesus immediately asked them the same question. "But who do you say that I am?". This time, Peter was the one to speak up decisively, "You are the Messiah, the Son of the living God."[23] Giussani observed that Peter answered "in his usual impulsive way [...] probably repeating something he had heard Jesus Himself say, although he had not fully grasped its significance."[24] Why did he do it? Why did Peter repeat the words that man had said about Himself? He repeated them and made them his because by then it was clear to him, after three years of living with Jesus, after the many signs that had happened, that if he could not trust that man, he could not even trust himself. Because of the certainty he had reached about Jesus, he accepted as true what He said about Himself. Here, this is faith: "to recognize that what a historical Presence says of itself is true,"[25] to adhere to His presence affirming as truth what He says. "Faith is an act of reason moved by the exceptional nature of a Presence that brings man to say, 'This man who is speaking is truthful. He is not lying, I accept what He says'."[26]

---

[23] Mt 16:15-16.
[24] L. Giussani, *At the Origin of the Christian Claim*, 71.
[25] L. Giussani-S. Alberto-J. Prades, *Generating Traces in the History of the World*, 16.
[26] *Ibid.*, 35.

Two thousand years later, we are in exactly the same situation. Just as Peter and the other friends dealt with the man Jesus of Nazareth, who was not a vision, but a man, so we too are dealing with the human reality in which Christ makes Himself present, with the companionship that is its Body in history, the Church, according to the face with which it has touched us. We too, through our experience of this companionship, through the human change we see documented in the people who belong to it with simplicity, through the gladness and gratuitousness we see flower in them, even with all the limits of each person, with the fragility and wretchedness of each person, we can say that "in our experience, there is something that comes from beyond it: unforeseeable, mysterious, but within our experience." "There is a factor within, a factor that decides about this companionship, certain outcomes of this companionship, certain resonances of this companionship, a factor so surprising that if I don't affirm something else I don't give reason to the experience, because reason is to affirm experiential reality according to all the factors that make it up, all of the factors. There can be a constitutive factor, of which we only feel a reverberation, of which we feel the fruit, of which we even see the consequences, but we aren't able to see this factor directly. If I say: 'So it doesn't exist,' I am mistaken, because I eliminate something of the experience–this is no longer reasonable."[27]

What instrument can we use to know this factor? With the intelligence of reality that we call faith.

[27] L. Giussani, *Is It Possible to Live This Way?*, Vol. 2, *Hope*, 103-104.

"Faith is a form of knowledge that is beyond the limit of reason," that "grasps something that reason cannot grasp." Faith, Giussani said, "is an act of knowledge that grasps the Presence of something that reason would not know how to grasp, but yet that reason has to affirm, otherwise something within experience would be lost, eliminated, something that experience *indicates*." "Reason cannot perceive 'the presence of Jesus among us,' 'Christ is here now,' the way it perceives that you are here. Do you understand? Yet, it cannot *not* admit the He is here."[28]

The problem of faith arises today as it did two thousand years ago with the same question, "Who is this man?" It is the question "that is born in the heart of those who, even if they do not articulate it, seeing a certain person or persons or a certain community or certain way of living, ask 'How can they be this way?'."[29] It is the implicit, unsaid question that barista asked about the university students who hung out at his cafe, but above all it is the question that emerged in us in front of the human reality we came up against. Each of us searches for our own answers. But if they cannot explain the human newness we see and participate in, it is reasonable and coherent with the whole journey we have made to open ourselves to the answer offered us (one we could not have conceived of on our own) by the living tradition of the Church, by the companionship encountered. "We are this way because Christ is present among us." The Church

---

[28] *Ibid*, 104-105.
[29] L. Giussani, *Si può (veramente?!) vivere così?* [Is It (Truly?!) Possible to Live This Way?], 130-131. Our translation.

proposes itself as the prolungation of Christ in space and time, as the place and the sign of His presence,[30] and we, like Peter, because of the exceptional things we have observed, the unimaginable correspondence we have experienced, the certainty we have attained, through the power of His graze, can recognize Christ present in this human reality; we can make ours the words that Peter was the first to pronounce.

e) So then, where does the shadow over the truth come from?

When someone has travelled this trajectory, as many among us have done, why does uncertainty still remain?

Often we attribute our uncertainty to a lack of signs or weakness of the evidence or our lack of coherence about the evidence we have perceived. But, as Giussani observed, "the shadow over the truth is not due to the lack of evidence and reason, but to the lack of affection for it, always, absolutely always. Because truth bears its evidence within; it wears it on its face." Truth is discovered "exactly the way you are surprised when a beautiful woman passes on the street. You say, 'How beautiful!' Truth has the same nature and immediacy, and there is no possibility of dialectic prevaricating: it is this way! Truth bears its evidence, the evidence of itself within, wears it on its face." Therefore the uncertainty that insinuates itself into our hearts "does not have good reasons." Its "direct object" is not the content of the announcement. Uncertainty is always

---

[30] Cfr. L. Giussani, *Why The Church?*, 206.

indirect; it is "the bother, the reluctance, the tiredness, the effort we will have to make in front of the certain truth that has crossed our horizon": uncertainty enters like a "lie" and "the lie is an ethical attitude," a position we take on, "not an act of the intelligence."[31]

There is no certainty in knowing without fondness for reality, without wonder and involvement of your affections, without "active sincerity"[32] in front of the object you are considering, without an *affectus*, moved emotion. "Knowledge involves affection, involves a repercussion that is called affection, *affectus*. Our soul is *touchée*, touched. True knowledge is the union of these two factors."[33]

A precious documentation of all this can be found in those "moments of people" when they are so absorbed by an event that they cannot block the affection for the truth that happens in front of them.

"Dear Julián, Monday during the meeting with university students, when you asked a person who had a question 'If Jesus came now and asked you, Do you love me? how would you answer?', I was moved to tears, and even before I could formulate words, my whole being cried 'Yes, I answer yes'. I felt a repercussion that left all the rest aside and filled me with the desire to yield to that 'yes.' This has not always been my reac-

---

[31] L. Giussani, *Uomini senza patria* [Men without a Homeland] *(1982-1983)*, 255-256. Our translation.

[32] L. Giussani, *The Religious Sense*, 32.

[33] L. Giussani, *Si può (veramente?!) vivere così?* [Is It (Truly?!) Possible to Live This Way?], 61. Evdokimov said, "For modern man the difficulty depends on the separation between intelligence and heart, between knowledge and judgement of value" (P. Evdokimov, *Le età della vita spirituale* [The Ages of Spiritual Life] (Bologna: Il Mulino, 1968), 219. Our translation from the Italian translation.

tion. It happened to me continually last year during the month when I was deciding whether to begin the journey of verification of a vocation to virginity. There were a lot of things I didn't understand and I was full of questions. Many times I doubted things I'd already acknowledged, but in front of the great things that were happening to me, the desire to be able to answer 'yes' exploded continually in me. It's something that emerges from me even before I can explain it; before I can set in order the facts, memories and thoughts, my person has already answered 'yes.' Starting from this, it becomes increasingly interesting to look over all the facts of my life from which that reaction and affection gushed, clarifying the history, the road, and in this way increasing my wonder and gratitude. For me, just the simple fact that the repercussion exists is already an index of the truth that happens and attracts me."

Those who have reached certainty about faith can face the question of hope. What is the source of hope?

2. Certainty of faith is the seed of certainty of hope

Péguy wrote: "To hope, my child, one must be very happy, one must have obtained, received great grace."[34] This emerges in the testimonies we have read: the happening of a grace that causes the heart to leap and that kindles hope.

[34] Ch. Péguy, *The Portico of the Mystery of the Second Virtue*, trans. Dorothy Brown Aspinwall (Metuchen: Scarecrow Press, 1970), 12.

What is the greatest grace we have received? The encounter with Christ, who "brought all newness by bringing Himself," the newness of each circumstance, of each relationship, of each situation. We have encountered a presence that made our heart leap. We have been looked upon with an unknown tenderness, embraced and forgiven beyond all imagination.

Those who have seen the newness that Christ brings into life, to the point of reaching a sure recognizion of His presence, will necessarily share Saint Paul's experience. "What then shall we say to this? If God is for us, who can be against us? He who did not spare His own Son but handed Him over for us all, how will He not also give us everything else along with Him? Who will bring a charge against God's chosen ones? It is God who acquits us. Who will condemn? It is Christ Jesus who died, rather, was raised, who also is at the right hand of God, who indeed intercedes for us. Who will separate us from the love of Christ? Will anguish, or distress, or persecution, or famine, or nakedness, or peril, or the sword? As it is written, '*For your sake we are being slain all the day; we are looked upon as sheep to be slaughtered.*' No, in all these things we conquer overwhelmingly through Him who loved us."[35]

Those who have experienced His companionship, who have acknowledged that He gave His life for us, look at everything with this Presence in their eyes. "For I am convinced that neither death, nor life, nor angels, nor principalities, nor present things, nor future things, nor power, nor height, nor depth, nor any

35 Rm 8:31-37.

other creature will be able to separate us from the love of God in Christ Jesus our Lord."[36]

So what is the source of hope? Hope is born of the recognition of Christ present in a human difference; it is like a flower of faith. It is simple. Think of a child's certainty about her mother, recognized as a good presence. The child cannot think about the future, the day to come, if not grounded in the certainty of the presence of her mother, the certainty that her mother will always be with her, no matter what happens. What holds for a child holds for each of us.

"Often my hope is that nothing bad will happen to us. I say, 'Let's hope,' expressing the generic and a bit superstitious confidence of a person who 'hopes' things will go well. But this position doesn't hold water, because in reality we are never safe from anything. Once I was talking to my seven-year-old daughter about the chance of seeing my parents, who live far away, and I'd exclaimed, 'Let's hope!". She perceived my skepticism about the possibility that it could happen, and said, 'Mamma, if you say you hope this way, it means you don't belive it." She was right. Hope has to do with a certainty. What certainty? What certainty do I need in order to hope? Certainty that no matter what happens to me and my loved ones, the darkness will not win, suffering and desperation will not win. This is the certainty I need now. My children are a living example of this. For them, life is always a present that looks to the future with assurance. They're not afraid of anything, except the dark. But they're serene because we are there. Well, what about me?"

[36] Rm 8:38-39.

We can think about the future in a positive way no matter what happens, only because of our recognition of Christ, this presence who has entered our lives through an encounter, and who never abandons us, as we had the opportunity to experience during the pandemic.

Almost without our realizing it, hope blossoms like a flower of the faith; it emerges from the certainty of Christ present, challenging any suspicion that may enter our hearts. "The great grace from which hope is born is the certainty of faith; the certainty of faith is the seed of the certainty of hope." So its growth happens as slowly as that of a seed. "The small seed that's planted today will only begin to come out in September of the coming year and only after four or five years does it begin to delineate itself as a little plant with those gentle and strange characteristics."[37]

In order to hope, "it is necessary to have received a great grace," the grace of certainty in the present. We can appreciate how crucial this is with even greater clarity in the present situation. "No one has certainty in the present; everyone has certainty in the present when they're not thinking of it; if they think about it … they have no certainty." Many might feel comforted by their money, career, or good health, but if asked about it seriously, it become evident how rare "true certainty with regard to the ultimate meaning of living" really is. And yet "it's certainty regarding the present, therefore of a meaning in the present that, in time, makes a place for a certainty regarding the future."[38]

"Ever since the beginning of this pandemic I was afraid because I've had a health problem for quite a while that classifies me among those 'at risk.' Last summer there was the belief that everything was a bit more under control, and with the news that vaccines were on the way, I said to myself, 'Ah, now I'm ok; I don't need to be afraid anymore.' I had placed my hope in the vaccine. Instead, everything was turned on its head shortly after, because I got pregnant and couldn't be vaccinated. (In line with the indications of the Italian healthcare authorities, I asked my doctor, and he said it would be risky.) Fortunately, my husband found a new job, but it didn't allow him to be at home as much as the previous year. In addition, during this new wave of Covid my city had the record numbers of infections. So then, I asked myself, 'where is my hope?'. During the day I ask this question often; it spurs me to do a work of verification in what happens and surrounds me. This question enables me to start fresh. For example, my husband and I are naturally timid and allow ourselves to become anxious, but at times it's enough for us to ask each other, 'Is there hope?', and we return to looking at something else, or better, Someone else who happened in our life and seized us, and so we ask Him, the One who is our hope! This has become a daily work of verification for us. An episode helped me understand the question of hope better. Recently our firstborn, disabled from birth, celebrated his eight birthday. That evening before eating the birthday cake,

[38] *Ivi.*

we asked our children to say a prayer that was different from the usual one: each person should give a reason for being thankful. The birthday boy said, 'I thank God for my existence, because I wanted to be born: I wanted to exist!'. Hearing those words, my husband and I looked at each other, thunderstruck. We thought of when I was pregnant with him and discovered he had a rare deformity. I thought of all the pressure from the doctors to interrupt the pregnancy, and also of our acquaintances who told us that bringing a child like that into the world would condemn him to unhappiness. Eight years later, that same child said those words, so strong and penetrating for my mother's heart. This shook and moved me so much that I, too, thanked God for the *yes* to his life that my husband and I said through grace. And I understood that there is hope! There is always hope, even in the most complicated situations because life and reality are positive; they are for a good! So even the coronavirus, the dramatic situations of difficulty and limitation cannot rob my hope and my ability to say that there is an ultimate positiveness in reality, because an Other makes it. An Other who is hidden in the appearances of things and who never abandons me, who has come to encounter me and holds me every day with tenderness through the gratuitous good of my husband and children, through the facts that happen and through this companionship of ours, which helps by telling me, 'Look, behind the clouds the sun is shining'."

This is the deep reason of the working hypothesis we gave ourselves for facing the pandemic: "Always living reality intensely." Those who followed it will be able to recognize that they have carried out the verification, because in their circumstances they find they have hope, as the friend who wrote the letter told us. Because of what everyone has had to live, we could ask ourselves whether these months have been a prison or an experience of freedom behind the "bars" of confinement, as it was for Cardinal Van Thuan.[39]

"Hope is certainty regarding the future that is based on the certainty about a present."[40] This is another way of conceiving hope, not imbalanced on an image of a future but centered on the certainty of a presence. Here the relationship with the future is entirely determined by the experience of One present. We can look at the future in a positive way only on the strength of a present that makes us experience this irreducible positiveness already. If the promise does not begin to be fulfilled now, it is not credible. The certainty of destiny is grounded in the certainty of a present. Thus the problem is to reach certainty about this "present." All the substance of hope is based on faith.

Those who have reached this certainty experience another way of facing even the most turbulent shocks.

"During the Christmas holidays our very young daughter was diagnosed with cancer. Every day I wake with a great weight on my heart, but as I become conscious, I entrust myself to God. Every morning I get on my knees again and start fresh from there, from the relationship with the Mystery. I don't know how I could live differently. Away from You, where would I go? I start fresh from the knowledge that

---

[39] Cf. T. Gutiérrez de Cabiedes, *Van Thuan. Libero tra le sbarre* [Free Behind Bars] (Rome: Città Nuova, 2018).

[40] L. Giussani, *Is It Possible to Live This Way?*, Vol. 2, *Hope*, 14.

I am a daughter and thus loved by a good Father. I realize in the moment that I am entirely needy, that everything is a gift and then I discover I'm grateful. Everything is amplified, my need for good for myself and toward everything. I look at the people I meet in the hospital and wish all of them could meet He who is the answer to their desire. For me it is the only road. Nothing distracts me from this wound that at moments is incomprehensible, but after two months I think it's more reasonable to abandon myself to this embrace of the Mystery who holds me close. Jesus is giving me my daughter to look at. After an operation, looking at some messages, she said, "A lot of people tell me, you'll see, it'll pass and later you'll be better, later you'll be healed, later, later… but I want to live now!'." For me, staying in the present means living with all my desire, which is not lost in lines of reasoning but becomes an insistent prayer of entreaty. I am always in a position of waiting: for bloodwork results, for treatment to begin, for the results of a CAT scan or PET, etc., but it is not an experience of suspension, because I live clinging to what happens, begging and waiting for Jesus. The more attentive I am to His signs, the more the present becomes livable and my affection for Him grows. Many people stop by to say hello, even if only a quick one, to see how it is possible to live such a circumstance without being buried by it. Everyone seeks Him and wants to see where He is victorious. I am really struck by this because I understand that I am nothing and He does everything, and so I look at them, who are looking at Him. I don't know how to explain it better, but our reciprocal companionship grows through this. Going to work doesn't distract me from what I am living, either: reality is complex and formed of many facets, but I feel unified because I always seek Him, be it at home, in the hospital, the office or the supermarket. Looking at myself in action, I discover I am more myself. Everything interests me. What a grace our road is, the way it makes us aware of our own particular story! It is worthwhile to travel this piece of the road without losing anything, because it has to do with me, with my destiny and everything has a weight, takes on eternal value, even if I don't understand everything, but this doesn't matter [This is living reality intensely!]. It scares me a bit to articulate it, but I sense that there is something even greater than the health of my daughter, even if naturally I never stop asking insistently for her healing from He who can do everything. If God looks at me this way, doesn't He love my daughter, who is His, just as much? His presence is my hope."

Religious sentimentality, which is so widespread among us as well, does not lead to the certainty that glows from the words we have just read, but, as I said, it is a journey that we choose to make, continually sustained by His living presence. Therefore, our boundless gratitude to Giussani grows, for his having untiringly testified about this journey to us and shown it to us.

"Even if your father or mother should abandon you, I will never abandon you."[41] Only this grounds our hope. When something happens that is equal to the drama of living, it also changes our gaze on the future. Not just any presence is the repository of our

[41] Cf. Is 49:15.

hope. We see this Presence when facts happen that challenge life.

What is the form of the fulfillment of our desire, the expectant awaiting that we are? Often we identify the fulfillment of our boundless expectancy with a particular image that, once achieved, disappoints us, as Pavese noted the day he received the Strega Prize. "In Rome, apotheosis. And with this?"[42] The form of fulfillment is not any of our images. The form of fulfillment and thus of hope is Christ Himself. But this is not a given that we can take for granted: nothing is less so, as documented in a letter from one of us.

"I see many people around me who are discouraged, who fear the pandemic and their own solitude, but without a doubt I also see people who, each in their own circumstances, live with a gladness and intensity that make them fascinating, now more than ever. Even so, it seems to me that certainty in the future is unattainable. That peace does not arrive, is not arriving yet, at least not the way I often picture it, like an immediately ready response to everything and as 'serenity.' Everything is always a struggle, full of doubts and dramatic intensity. Maybe this is what Augustine meant when he wrote, 'My heart is restless until it rests in Thee,' but I'm not sure I can love this restlessness. Maybe my idea of what 'certainty in the future' means is still immature, because the restlessness lacks a 'sure point' as I imagine it, and rather than being a powerful tool for inquiry, turns into something threatening and irritating. So I tend to suppress it with ephemeral things (I put my work in order, so I'll feel more tran-

---

[42] See here, pp. 80-81.

quil; I maintain peace in the family because it's the right thing to do; I buy a bigger house so that we'll be better set up for the next pandemic, and in any case it can serve as a gathering place for friends...), expecting these things to be a solution for the request of my heart. But after a while they all leave me the way I was before, or maybe a bit more cynical. Or I tend to do pious gestures, but my volunteering performance does not give me certainty in the future: if the final result, the outcome depends on some capacity of mine, it is vulnerable. There is always a final leap into the void that I have to take, and that certainty never arrives. What is the missing step? What enables a present reality to become certainty in the future and to win over the heart?"

The tenth leper understood this well. As soon as he was healed from his leprosy, he did not settle for the healing, but felt the urgent need to return to Jesus.[43] He understood that his expectancy was not fulfilled once he was healed, and that Jesus was the one to fulfill it. Maybe the fact that he was Samaritan made it easier for him not to take the healing for granted. He could not expect any favors from anyone. This made him appreciate even more both the healing and above

---

[43] "As He continued His journey to Jerusalem, He traveled through Samaria and Galilee. As He was entering a village, ten lepers met Him. They stood at a distance from him and raised their voice, saying 'Jesus, Master! Have pity on us!' And when He saw them, He said, 'Go show yourselves to the priests.' As they were going they were cleansed. And one of them, realizing he had been healed, returned, glorifying God in a loud voice; and he fell at the feet of Jesus and thanked Him. He was a Samaritan. Jesus said in reply, 'Ten were cleansed, were they not? Where are the other nine? Has none but this foreigner returned to give thanks to God?' Then he said to him, 'Stand up and go; your faith has saved you.' (Lk 17:11-19).

all the unique correspondence he experienced in that Presence, and he did not want to lose it. Joy, fulfillment and fullness were in the relationship with Him. "That they should know You, the only true God, and the one whom you sent, Jesus Christ,"[44] this is eternal life, or in other words, life-life, the only thing that corresponds to the expectant awaiting.

The form of the response to our expectancy is Christ Himself, "His sweet presence," as we often sing in *Jesu dulcis memoria*.[45] Saint Augustine expressed it with the invitation to "let the Lord your God be your hope. Hope for nothing else from the Lord your God; but let the Lord your God Himself be your hope."[46] Hugh of Saint Victor said it in another way. He "comes not to fulfill desire but to attract affection."[47] In everything we enjoy, He comes to evoke the question, 'But don't you miss Me?'".

The content of the verification we have been able to do in this long recent period with all the dramatic situations and trials it has caused and causes, is not whether we have consolidated a discourse or can repeat it by heart, but whether our affection for Christ has grown, whether Christ attracted our entire person and we, too, like Peter, can say "All my preference as

---

[44] Jn 17:3.

[45] "*Jesu dulcis memoria*," Gregorian hymn, XII century, in *Canti* [Songs] (Milan: Soc. Coop. Ed. Nuovo Mondo, 2014), 23-24.

[46] Saint Augustine, *Enarrationes in Psalmos* 40,7 [Exposition on Psalm 40]. Available in English at https://www.newadvent.org/fathers/1801040.htm

[47] Cf. Hugh of Saint Victor, *De arra anime. L'inizio del dono* [The Beginning of the Gift] (Milan: Glossa, 2000), 1. Our translation from the Italian translation.

a man is for You, Christ!". This is the only thing that counts.

If His presence is our fullness, asking for this presence is the form of Christian hope: *Veni Sancte Spiritus.* "Come, Lord Jesus!"[48] is the invocation that closes the Bible, because His presence is the one thing that constantly satisfies and exalts the desire of our heart. We can recognize whether our affection for Christ has grown if it is He who is missing in every thing we enjoy, and not because we have not encountered Him, but precisely because having encountered Him, we have an uncontainable desire to see Him every day, to seek Him every day, no longer able to live without Him!

So then, let us ask that Paul's prayer be realized in our life, "that the God of our Lord Jesus Christ [...] give you a spirit of wisdom and revelation resulting in knowledge of Him. May the eyes of your hearts be enlightened, that you may know what is the hope that belongs to His call." [49]

[48] Rev. 22:20.
[49] Eph 1:17-18.

CHAPTER 5

THE NOURISHMENT OF HOPE

"The Church never takes faith for granted."[1] The same can be said of hope (and this explains why the two sins against hope are presumption and despair).[2]

Faith and hope are not achieved once and for all; they are constantly challenged by events and circumstances, as documented by the experiences of many among us.

1. The struggle of the journey

A friend wrote me, "The question in my heart today is this: many times I've experienced that hope exists, but in front of the trials that my life forces me to undergo, my legs tremble. I ask myself: I know that hope exists, but do I not believe it deep down? Do I have little faith? How can I start fresh every morning with the

---

[1] Francis, Encyclical Letter, *Lumen fidei*, 6.

[2] "The first commandment is also concerned with sins against hope, namely, despair and presumption: By *despair*, man ceases to hope for his personal salvation from God, for help in attaining it or for the forgiveness of his sins. Despair is contrary to God's goodness, to His justice–for the Lord is faithful to His promises–and to His mercy. There are two kinds of *presumption*. Either man presumes upon his own capacities, (hoping to be able to save Himself without help from on high), or he presumes upon God's almighty power or His mercy (hoping to obtain His forgiveness without conversion and glory without merit)." (*Catechism of the Catholic Church*, 2091-2092).

certainty that there is hope? It seems like the encounter I've had isn't enough, even if it was very important and it generated me." Thank God it isn't enough! Like all of us, you need it to happen now. Precisely because everything that has happened to you is so important for generating the person you are now, every morning you can look at the day as a crucial part of the journey you still have to travel for the increase of your faith, the rediscovery of His presence, the one foundation of our hope. Therefore, the adventure begins every morning, and thank God, I would add, because if I were spared struggle and toil, I could not see the victory of Christ happen again, which I need now for living.

Another person observed, "This year I got work in a public school and I've met some new colleagues, many of them very experienced and knowledgeable, who're teaching me a great deal. With a certain wonder I've seen an underlying despair in them. On the one hand, I understand it because it comes from the deep questions about what we're going through or the illness of people dear to them. On the other hand, I perceive that theirs is a real despair, the feeling of rolling toward nothingness, that isn't the case for me. It's not that I'm particularly cheerful, but I see in myself a final bulwark that holds up and doesn't allow the wave of nothingness to overwhelm me. It's something "I am" and not something I know how to do. I can only think that it comes from the encounter that seized me, because this is the only difference between me and them. I find hope in myself without having done anything to deserve it, but I understand that it won't remain automatically and that it isn't there for life: I have to rediscover it. I need to clarify this point because in the current situation I see in myself and others a darkening, a weariness and difficulty."

Paradoxically, the fact that it does not automatically remain is precisely what forces us to rediscover the content of our hope, to overcome the darkening. Pope Francis described this existential situation in his testimony the evening of March 27, 2020 in Saint Peter's Square. "When evening had come" (*Mk* 4:35). The Gospel passage we have just heard begins like this. For weeks now it has been evening. Thick darkness has gathered over our squares, our streets and our cities; it has taken over our lives, filling everything with a deafening silence and a distressing void, that stops everything as it passes by; we feel it in the air, we notice in people's gestures, their glances give it away. We find ourselves afraid and lost. Like the disciples in the Gospel we were caught off guard by an unexpected, turbulent storm. We have realized that we are on the same boat, all of us fragile and disoriented, but at the same time important and needed, all of us called to row together, each of us in need of comforting the other. On this boat… are all of us. Just like those disciples, who spoke anxiously with one voice, saying "We are perishing" (v. 38).[3]

We too, like the disciples, are challenged by events that crash over us like waves from every direction. Human life is a journey, a struggle, "like a voyage on the sea of history, often dark and stormy."[4] It is a struggle not only because of the challenges of circum-

---

[3] Francis, *Extraordinary moment of prayer*, Sagrato of St. Peter's Basilica, March 27, 2020.
[4] Benedict XVI, Encyclical letter *Spe salvi*, 49.

stances but also because of the very nature of human experience, the drama it holds, as well described in the story told by Martin Buber and quoted by Joseph Ratzinger in *Introduction to Christianity*.

"An adherent of the Enlightenment [writes Buber], a very learned man, who had heard of the Rabbi of Berditchev, paid a visit to him in order to argue, as was his custom, with him, too, and to shatter his old-fashioned proofs of the truth of his faith. When he entered the Rabbi's room, he found him walking up and down with a book in his hand, rapt in thought. The Rabbi paid no attention to the new arrival. Suddenly he stopped, looked at him fleetingly, and said, 'But perhaps it is true after all.' The scholar tried in vain to collect himself–his knees trembled, so terrible was the Rabbi to behold and so terrible his simple utterance to hear. But rabbi Levi Yitschak now turned to face him and spoke quite calmly: 'My son, the great scholars of the Torah with whom you have argued wasted their words upon you; as you departed, you laughed at them. They were unable to lay God and His Kingdom on the table before you, and neither can I. But think, my son, perhaps it is true.' The exponent of the Enlightenment opposed him with all his strength; but this terrible 'perhaps' that echoed back at him time after time broke his resistance."[5]

Up to this point Buber's story. Ratzinger commented: "That 'perhaps' is the unavoidable temptation it [unbelief] cannot elude, the temptation in which it, too, in the very act of rejection, has to experience the

---

[5] M. Buber, *Tales of the Hasidim*, in J. Ratzinger, *Introduction to Christianity* (San Francisco: Comunio Books, Ignatius Press, 2004), 46.

unrejectability of belief. In other words, both the believer and the unbeliever share, each in his own way,
doubt *and* belief, if they do not hide from themselves
and from the truth of their being. Neither can quite
escape either doubt or belief; for the one, faith is present *against* doubt; for the other, *through* doubt and
in the *form* of doubt. It is the basic pattern of man's
destiny only to be allowed to find the finality of his
existence in this unceasing rivalry between doubt and
belief, temptation and certainty. Perhaps in precisely
this way doubt, which saves both sides from being
shut up in their own worlds, could become the avenue
of communication. It prevents both from enjoying
complete self-satisfaction; it opens up the believer to
the doubter and the doubter to the believer; for one, it
is his share in the fate of the unbeliever; for the other,
the form in which belief remains nevertheless a challenge to him."[6]

The stakes in the question of faith and hope are the
highest possible, because in the final analysis they regard the alternative between being and nothingness,
"whether existence ends in the dust of passing time,
and its passing is nothing other than the construction
of a tomb or prison where we will suffocate and die
uselessly, or whether time is pregnant with the future,
and every moment carries the weight of eternity, as
Ada Negri said." On the one hand, "absolute nothingness, the nothingness of nothingness" and on the
other hand, "responsibility for eternity, in front of the
eternal." And the "I," our "I," your "I," my "I," is the
"crossroads between being and nothingness," forced

[6] J. Ratzinger, *Introduction to Christianity*, 47-48.

every morning "to choose between an everything that ends in nothingness [...] and life that has a purpose."[7]

Perhaps the recent challenges have made us discover this like no time in the past. We have felt united in the difficulties, people of faith and nonbelievers. In responding to the circumstances, believers verify their faith in front of everyone, including nonbelievers. They discover whether faith makes them substantial in front of the trials and questions of living. Thus also nonbelievers become travelling companions for believers, and believers, in turn, with their testimony, participate in the destiny of nonbelievers.

The words of Lucía Méndez capture a widespread and transversal situation. We are thrown "into the darkness of the present, immersed up to our necks in uncertainty [...] mourning the endless numbers of the dead, and desirous of seeing some sign of normalcy on the road."[8] Beyond explicitly assumed positions, the different itineraries and points of arrival, an appeal has returned to the heart and lips of many, perhaps like an echo of a directly or indirectly received education, as Joana Bonet wrote. "Our Father, who art in heaven [...] Today it would be of comfort to know whether you are looking at us from the stars, from Mars or from the infinite itself; that you are moved by our baying, our animal solitude [...] We have never looked up this way from our window or balcony [...] Deliver us from evil. It has always been the best sen-

---

[7] L. Giussani, *Attraverso la compagnia dei credenti* [Through the companionship of the believers] (Milan: Bur, 2021), 19, 31. Our translation.

[8] L. Méndez, "Sin tregua y sin pudor," *El Mundo*, January 9, 2021. Our translation from the Italian translation.

tence of the Our Father, that prayer that continues to be prayed like a universal glue, even among those who do not believe or believe in that way."[9]

The writer Silvia Avallone recounted that the second wave of the pandemic caught her unprepared, like a sudden incursion that gave her no chance to barricade inside herself. Seeing her daughter play in the park, she opened in her own way to the "perhaps" described by Ratzinger. "When the infection curve and the number of deaths began to rise again, businesses closed, the blood froze in my veins. I felt stupid, fooled by my own naivety. [...] All of us, we human beings, are not equipped for the void. As soon as we experience one, we immediately feel the need to fill it as soon as possible [...]. We are no longer children and we cannot return to being so. What comes naturally to them costs us immense difficulty: accepting reality for what it is, adhering to it, digging deep to find a stone, a shriveled flower, any reason for hanging on and going forward: a hope. However, in this moment, going against our instinct as adults seems to me to be the only gesture that makes sense."[10]

Echoing observations we proposed at the beginning of our itinerary, Mario Vargas Llosa, winner of the 2010 Nobel Prize for Literature, said recently, "The pandemic surprised everyone because we had the impression that science and technology had dominated nature. We were shocked to discover that this was not

[9] J. Bonet, "Padrenuestro," *La Vanguardia*, April 8, 2020. Our translation from the Italian translation.
[10] S. Avallone, "Resistere affidandosi ai tesori di ogni giorno [Hanging on, entrusting ourselves to everyday treasures]." *Corriere della Sera*, December 28, 2020, p. 5. Our translation.

true. We saw how the unexpected can lead us to the abyss. Now we wonder how and when all this will end and what the consequences will be. The world will become very different from how it was at the beginning of this story. And then there is an economic crisis that will hit many. We have been subjected to a violent quake during what seemed like progress toward prosperity and freedom. All this has left us disconcerted. Maybe it's not a bad thing to face reality less optimistically."[11]

We could go on and on, but the point is clear: nobody is spared reality with everything it entails, neither believers nor nonbelievers. The experience of daily living and the news show us this nonstop.

2. The dwelling place of the Most High

The same thing happened to the people of Israel, whose faith in God did not spare them any of the adversities of history. Believing is not like getting a full vaccination, as we might like to think. This is a reduced image of faith. No vaccine can make us immune to the difficulties of life. The whole history of the people of Israel testifies to this.

The beginning of the people of Israel was the covenant established between God and Abraham. "I am God the Almighty. Walk in My presence and be blameless. Between you and Me I will establish My

[11] M. Vargas Llosa, "La 'ley Celaá' es un disparate absoluto," interview by P.G. Cuartango, *ABC*, January 17, 2021. Our translation from the Italian translation.

covenant, and I will multiply you exceedingly."[12] Even so, this covenant was put to the test by the unforeseen events and adverse circumstances of history. So, we might ask, does having faith and hope make no difference? Is life the same for those who have faith and hope and for those who do not? There certainly is a difference, and how! It does not lie in the quantity or quality of the challenges, but in the different way of facing them, according to the newness brought by a God who entered history and made the descendents of Abraham into His people, a peope who had Someone to turn to when faced by needs and adversities, to be sustained in hope.

Moses understood this. Having seen God face to face and having found grace in His eyes did not spare him from having to face all the challenges that appeared along the road to the Promised Land. In his novel *Desert*, Jan Dobraczyński gave us a vivid portrayal of the journey of Moses and the people of Israel, none of which was taken for granted or linear. Therefore Moses said to the Lord, "'If You are not going Yourself, do not make us go up from here.' […] The Lord said to Moses: 'This request, too, which you have made, I will carry out, because you have found favor with Me and you are My intimate friend'."[13] But it seemed that not even God's promise to accompany them and the prodigies they saw at the very beginning of their journey, with the defeat of Pharoh's army, were enough. Quite soon the fragility of their trust in the presence of the Lord began to emerge. The

[12] Gen 17:1-2.
[13] Ex 33:15,17.

lack of food made them regret leaving the onions of Egypt. So God responded to their hunger quickly with mannah. But this was not enough either. "The people began to spit on the mannah and demand meat. Their cries echoed so stubbornly that Moses suddenly felt he could no longer bear the weight."[14] God intervened again. "The Lord answered Moses: 'Is this beyond the Lord's reach? You shall see now whether or not what I have said to you takes place'."[15] At that point, "there arose a wind from the Lord that drove in quail from the sea and left them all around the camp site, so a distance of a day's journey and at a depth of two cubits upon the ground. So all that day, all night, and all the next day the people set about to gather in the quail."[16]

Notwithstanding all the signs, their fragility in faithfulness emerged time after time in history. Instead of hoping in the Lord, who brought them out of Egypt, who led them through the desert and gave them the gift of the land promised to Abraham, the people continually yielded to the temptation to seek the safety of their own hope elsewhere, in the idols they built or in alliances with other and more powerful peoples. Time after time the illusory character of those attempts became evident. Isaiah wrote:

"We look for light, but there is darkness;
for brightness, and we walk in gloom!
Like those who are blind we grope along the wall,
like people without eyes we feel our way.

---

[14] J. Dobraczyński, *Deserto. Il romanzo di Mosè* [Desert. The Novel of Moses] (Brescia: Morcelliana, 1993), 225-226. Our translation.
[15] Num 11:23.
[16] Num 11:31-32.

We stumble at midday as if at twilight,
among the vigorous, we are like the dead.
Like bears we all growl,
like doves we moan without ceasing.
We cry out for justice, but it is not there;
for salvation, but it is far from us.[17]

In front of the difficulties, the weakness of the people's hope was all too evident. If it had not been continually sustained by the prophets, it would have collapsed. Signs from the past were not enough. The history of the past was not enough to sustain hope in the present. Constant renewal of support was needed. It is not hard to understand the situation of the people of Israel, given our own experience and the perception of our own weakness!

Probably the most powerful challenge to the hope of the people of Israel was the Babylonian exile. They had lost the three great gifts of the Lord: the land, the monarchy and the temple. Where was their God? The exile was crucial for the faith of Israel because it showed the difference between the God of Abraham and the other gods. When other peoples were defeated, they abandoned their god because it was not powerful enough to free them from defeat. Instead, the God of Israel was not defeated by the defeat of the people. What experience of God must Israel have had to make them stay attached to Him even in exile? The difference of their God was seen in the hope He evoked.

As we said, hope needs the grounding of a presence that is more powerful than any fragility, a presence that never disappears. "God is our refuge and our

17 Is 59:9-11.

strength, / an ever-present help in distress." This could be an empty line, and yet for the Jewish people it was full of a lived and re-lived experience. The psalm continues: "Thus we do not fear, though earth be shaken / and mountains quake to the depths of the sea,/ though its waters rage and foam / and mountains totter at its surging." Why this security, this absence of fear? Because "streams of the river gladden the city of God, / the holy dwelling of the Most High. / God is in its midst; it shall not be shaken: / God will help it at break of day. / Though nations rage and kingdoms totter, / He utters His voice and the earth melts. […] / Come and see the works of the Lord."[18]

3. The place of hope

The place of hope is this "dwelling"–"the holy dwelling of the Most High. / God is in its midst; it shall not be shaken." In the Christian announcement, this dwelling is a man: Jesus of Nazareth, God made flesh, a man who walked the streets, who you could meet and with whom you could spend time. With Him even the most painful and difficult circumstances of life could be faced with unimaginable certainty of good, with surprising peace. "It is I. Do not be afraid."[19] Therefore, for those who followed Him, He became in time the rock upon which their whole person was founded, the factor of their hope. Knowing well the weakness of His disciples, Jesus promised that He would not leave

[18] Psalm 46:2-9.
[19] Jn 6:20.

them orphaned and alone in the midst of the storms they would have to face. "And behold, I am with you always, until the end of the age."[20]

How? With what method? "As the method of His continuity in history Christ chose a companionship: the Church, with a head, Saint Peter. A companionship in which His presence could be experienced, could be visible and touchable."[21] What is the Church made of? Of you and me. Giussani explained that "seizing us in Baptism, Christ *set us together as members of the same body* (cf. chapters 1-4 of the Letter to the Ephesians). He is present here and now, in me, through me, and the first expression of the change in which His presence is documented is that I recognize that I am united with you, that *we are one thing only*."[22] Therefore salvation, which is Him, the Mystery made flesh, emerges "in a human place, the origin of which is deeper than any historical inquiry or description. It flows from the Mystery, but we come up against this salvation in a human place."[23]

Our humanity grows through immanence in this place, through a journey that accompanies us all our lives.

One of you wrote, "I have realized that without hope you can't stay in front of certain open wounds; you can only look for distraction and turn away your gaze. One day an 82-year-old friend told me on the phone, 'I don't know how, because I feel all the aches and pains

20 Mt 28:20.
21 L. Giussani, *L'avvenimento cristiano* [The Christian Event], 60. Our translation.
22 *Ibid.*, 39-40.
23 *Ibid.*, 53.

of old age and I live alone, but I have never felt so ac-companied within the Movement as I do now. There is a continual richness of proposal, and I'm helped incredibly by the work we're doing in our School of Community group.' I was moved. Where can some-thing like this happen? Only in a place where Christ works continually and makes us certain. So hope takes us by the hand and sustains us. I wouldn't know how to say it differently. I live continually generated by His gaze that reaches me through your gaze, Julián, and slowly but surely through that of all the friends who follow the charism today. I wouldn't be able to give myself certainty or hope on my own."

Another person wrote, "In this recent period I've felt a great sense of powerlessness. I'm a nurse and I've always worked in the Covid ward. It's been so hard, and at a certain point I felt the need to put all the diffi-culties in play in the one place I feel truly understood– this companionship. We organized a meeting open to all the nurses to share our questions. I left it filled with wonder, comforted in all the difficulties and support-ed in my dramatic situation. The next day, entering the ward, I saw a colleague, someone who is always impeccable in everything, who looked at me and said, 'Often when I get home in the evening I vomit, be-cause all we're seeing seems to have no meaning, and because of the huge workload demanded of us.' I was silent for a moment, because I had felt her same cry of weariness, but I was tired, not in despair. I won-dered why. I'm no different from her. I remembered the meeting of the day before, reminding me 'You're not alone with your weariness and pain.' With that embrace in mind, I asked her if we could work together that day, because I needed her. Usually each person handles her own patients on her own, but that day we worked together in a way that had never happened before."

This is what we need, a *place* where we can return without being scandalized by anything, one that cannot be reduced to our own measures and "interpretations," that sustains our hope. We are led into this place through a certain encounter that attracts us and makes it evident that Christ is present and alive. "Christ takes hold of man in Baptism; He makes him grow and become an adult. And in an encounter He causes him to experience the fact that a new human reality is close to him, one that corresponds, convinces, educates, and is creative, and that strikes him in some way."[24] This encounter leads us into a companionship, not just any one, but the human companionship generated by His Spirit, in the Church.

The event of Christ goes on being present in history through the companionship of the believers, effective sign of the salvation of Christ for women and men. "This is how the risen Christ holds us in His embrace; this companionship [...] is the body of Christ that becomes present, so that we touch Him, we see Him, we feel Him. The value of this companionship is deeper than appearances, because what we see is the emergence of the Mystery of Christ revealing itself." He continued, "The companionship through which Christ embraces us makes us know better who Christ is. It reveals to us what He is for us. Jesus Christ is

[24] L. Giussani-S. Alberto-J. Prades, *Generating Traces in the History of the World*, 71.

present here and now. He goes on being present in history through the uninterrupted succession of men who belong to Him through the action of His Spirit, as members of His Body, the prolungation of His Presence in time and space."[25]

Jesus' continued presence in history is the most important issue for our heart as humans, for the certainty of our destiny and fulfillment, which it is impossible not to desire, whatever way we imagine it and whatever name we give it. In fact, the certainty of our fulfillment lies "in the objectivity of the history with which God made Himself present, therefore in the definitive form with which that history personally involved and guided us." Our fundamental hope cannot be in what we do and our attempts, which arrive as far as they arrive, or our utopias, but "in something so tremendously present that it challenged and challenges what we can create and that the others [...] can assure us." Our great hope is in the "Power that became Presence in history, time and space," and that is hidden today in the fragility of our flesh, so much so that "all it takes is being proud or impatient to live within it but not realize it; all it takes is a puff of breath from us to destroy everything. Instead, our richness is precisely the mystery present in that fragility."[26]

Our hope lives in a place where you see that your heart is rekindled and enlivened, where you experience concretely that your own limits are not the final

[25] *Ibid.*, 31.
[26] L. Giussani, *Alla ricerca del volto umano* [In Search of the Human Face], 98.

word. Giussani expressed this beautifully. "There is a place, an instrument, in which [...] the victorious Christ is a recognizable, perceived, experienced companionship that gives substance to life, a presence that is a continual root, an endless source–as He told the Samaritan woman at the well–of hope: our communion, our vocational companionship, people who together are called by nothing other than His Spirit. No matter how much the substance of this motivation was fragile and almost unconscious in the beginning, it is the one reason we know each other–the only one!–and there is no other. This is the instrument for knowing the risen Christ, the event that transmits, carries within the meaning of everything and that is present like my siblings and my mother."[27]

With Him in our eyes we can challenge any situation, beyond our imagining. Those among us who hope–*in spem contra spem* [hoping against hope]–[28] because they participate in the "mystery of this Mystical Body of Christ"[29] and cling to it, experience a new attraction of hope and with it security and industrious dynamism even in the most arduous and dramatic conditions. We have had many examples in this period, even where it seemed impossible. Commenting live during Pope Francis' journey to Iraq, [Italian journalist] Domenico Quirico said, "The one hope for those lands is to see in action another logic than that of hatred, revenge and sectarian violence.

---

[27] L. Giussani, *Una strana compagnia* [A Strange Companionship] (Milan: Bur, 2017), 81-82. Our translation.

[28] Rm 4:18.

[29] L. Giussani, *Porta la speranza. Primi scritti* [Bring Hope. Earliest Writings] (Genoa: Marietti *1820*, 1997), 160. Our translation.

In the Irachi Christians, persecuted Christians, we have seen the affirmation of another logic of living: the Christians are those who were subjected to evil, who accepted even martyrdom, without reacting and taking up arms. None of them took up arms. This is another world. This is a concrete hope for everyone and not just for the Christians.[30]

Across the world the same thing is happening in a different situation of trials. "I'm a cook, I live in Venezuela and belong to the community of the Movement. Struck by the question 'Is there hope?' I look at my experience and say 'yes, there is hope,' notwithstanding everything happening in my country. Perhaps you have no idea of everything that is lacking here. Our quality of life is terrible: without electricity, without water, unable to buy medicine, unable to go to a doctor because it's too expensive, getting up every morning worried about what we will eat. You can imagine the difficulty of living with a monthly salary of three dollars. We are weighed down by stress and anxiety in the midst of the Covid pandemic. But I want to tell you that with all this, there is hope, because there is a Presence made up of concrete faces, a companionship made up of space and time, affection and aid, that continually sets life back into motion. With all we're going through here, I've never felt alone. The encounter that God granted me has made it clear how Christ can enter our life and generate a change in humanity. I've begun looking differently at what we are going

---

[30] Domenico Quirico, *La Stampa* correspondent, speaking to *TV2000*, March 7, 2021. Our translation.

through, being more aware of the presence of Jesus, more attentive to each sign, more ready to say *yes*."

4. How do you recognize this place?

But how do you recognize this place that sustains our hope? First of all, as shown by our experience, we are not the ones to establish it. "It is the gift of the Holy Spirit that establishes and determines for each of us the concrete dwelling place in the Church, a human companionship that makes the journey to destiny more persuasive." In fact, the Event of Christ happens and attracts us according to "a specific form of time and space that enables us to face it in a certain way and makes it more understandable, more persuasive and more educationally effective." This characteristic of the intervention of the Spirit of Christ is called *charism*: it "provokes the Event existentially in a time and space." This gift of the charity of God is what makes possible faith, the awareness of the presence of Christ. Therefore, "In order that the Church, made up of men whom Christ has taken hold of and made part of His Body in Baptism, be an operatively effective reality in the world, men have to become aware of what has happened, aware of the encounter that Christ has had with them, and operate on the basis of that awareness."[31]

"I grew up in the Movement until, for a series of reasons, I decided to break off. This summer two

[31] L. Giussani-S. Alberto-J. Prades, *Generating Traces in the History of the World*, 78-79.

Student Youth [which gathers high school students in CL] girls who weren't even big friends of mine invited me to study with them for the Medical School entrance exam and then to go on holiday together in the mountains for a week. Spending time with them, I immediately realized that these two people and also their friends who joined us didn't look at my limitations, but looked at me and loved me just as I was and am." If our young friend immediately grasped this difference of gaze, experiencing the repercussion, it must be because she didn't find anything comparable elsewhere. She continued, "When I began university I perceived the same gaze in other CLU young people and so I decided to trust and follow them, going to School of Community and the gestures of the Movement. Spending time with them, I have felt loved and even the parts I like least about myself were embraced. With them, I realized I can ask my questions and take them seriously. In sum, I discovered hope for a possibility of life and a way of being together that I had not seen years before. The enthusiasm passed quickly and the difficulties of everyday life began to weigh on me, but it remained evident that in all these people I've met, there is hope. While I'm certain of the existence and tangible presence of this hope, I wonder how it can become mine, and how I can entrust myself completely to it."

Our friend came to a certain recognition of the tangible presence of a great hope in "these people I've met" notwithstanding their limits and fragility. But she does not settle for seeing it in others. She wants it to become hers, and asks how to entrust herself completely to it. The things she said indicate a journey that is worth highlighting here. "So I decided to trust and follow them." Let's ask ourselves about the reasons for trust and following.

When can we trust a place or person, such that in following we are rational and coherent with ourselves, particularly if the questions of life or death, our existence, the alternative between being and nothingness are at stake?

Giussani offers us three criteria. First of all, you have adequate reason to trust a person to the point of following and obeying her or him if "you see clearly in the conception of life that is explained and communicated to you that the actions of the person and the grounding of the person are based on the needs of the heart, both yours and of all people." Secondly, you have reason to trust "if the person gives you adequate help" and thirdly, "if the person does it gratuitously, caring for your good, such that the first strange thing that strikes you encountering the person is this aspect of gratuitousness." In this case, obeying this person is "fitting and right, as it is right to do what is rational."[32] Let's try to develop the three-fold criteria proposed.

First of all, as we said, it is rational to follow and obey another person "when this person communicates and reveals to me a conception of life and its destiny that *is entirely based on the original needs of the heart* that are common to all people."[33] Thus in order to recognize who it is reasonable to follow, you need an alert and awake "I" that is aware of its own original needs. In

---

[32] L. Giussani, *Si può (veramente?!) vivere così?* [Is It (Really?!) Possible to Live This Way?], 221-222. Our translation.
[33] *Ibid.*, 220.

fact, the consciousness of these needs is what enables us to perceive a reality that is pertinent to them, the place that brings a hope worthy of life. Therefore, in order not to fall prey to confusion and go after the first thing that passes, it is necessary to have "an attentive, tender, and impassioned awareness of my own self."[34]

In the second place, you can entrust yourself to a person who gives you adequate and appropriate help, who helps you to "overcome what is contrary to these needs, who helps you to sacrifice, understood as that aspect of awareness through which, adhering to the needs of the heart, you understand that you should give up or lose something."[35] It is difficult to face this appearance of loss and to accept the sacrifice required in many moments, without adequate help that is expressed in the presence of certain people. In this regard, there is a memorable passage by Fr. Giussani. "The waves are breaking in during a storm, but you have a voice next to you reminding you about reason, urging you not to let yourself be carried away by the billows, not to yield. The companionship tells you, 'Look, afterwards the sun will shine. You're in the midst of the waves now but later you'll come out and you'll see the sun.' Above all it tells you, 'Look.' Because in every vocational companionship there are always *people* or *moments of people* to look at. In the companionship, the most important thing is *to look* at people. Therefore the companionship is a great

[34] L. Giussani, *At the Origin of the Christian Claim*, 6.
[35] L. Giussani, *Si può (veramente?!) vivere così?* [Is It (Really?!) Possible to Live This Way?], 221. Our translation.

source of friendship. Friendship is defined by its purpose: help to walk toward destiny."[36]

The true help and goal of a companionship, of a friend, is not to spare us the relationship with reality but to support us in living it. Here our "I" is also in play. In fact, how often we ask for a kind of help that is not help at all! So then you need to distinguish. It is one thing to ask for a place that defends us from reality and helps us avoid it, exonerating us from the difficulty involved in facing it; it is another thing to ask that it introduce us to reality, whatever it may be. For that matter, Giussani observed, "if the Church were to proclaim that its aim was to take over the human effort of self-advancement, self-expression, and human searching, it would be acting like the kind of parents [...] who are deluded into thinking that they can resolve their children's problems by taking their place." But in this way the Church would fall short of her educational task, which "is not to provide man with solutions to the problems he encounters on his way,"[37] but to promote the right attitude in front of reality, as the optimal condition for facing problems, seeking where possible the solution.

Finally, it is reasonable to trust a person if the one motive for telling me certain things is care about my destiny, the gladness of my life, my happiness. "Not that we lord it over your faith; rather, we work together for your joy, for you to stand firm in the faith,"[38] said

[36] L. Giussani, *Un avvenimento di vita, cioè una storia* [A Life Event, i.e. a History], 459. Our translation.
[37] L. Giussani, *Why the Church?*, 155.
[38] 2 Cor 1:24.

Saint Paul. In other words, it is reasonable to trust a person if that person's motivation is not calculation, personal benefit, or policy, but gratuitousness. "Gratuitousness is love for the destiny of the other, nothing else." The people who communicate those things that correspond to the heart "do so without calculating anything, without having anything for themselves," but only so that "my life will have a good outcome, so that my life will reach its destiny." Once again, a vigilant and attentive "I" is required here. In fact, Giussani added, "Let's put this [...] very important factor in parentheses because it's not something you understand right away. You must have loved gratuitously for a long time, you must have been educated by life to love people gratuitously, in order to understand when a person loves you gratuitously."[39]

When we encounter people who have these characteristics that make it reasonable to follow them, we must follow them, out of coherence with ourselves. "Adhering to yourself means following the other: this is a paradox, the paradox that made Eve yield. Since the beginning of humankind, this is the paradox that is the proof of freedom: in order to be myself I must follow an other (as it will be among us)." Just imagine where you would be today if you had not followed this law. "This is the first thing that corresponds to the heart: I did not exist. If I want to exist I must follow an other. And those who speak to me of the human person in this way are right. Instead, those who speak to me of people as lords of their own destiny, capable of

---

[39] L. Giussani, *Si può (veramente?!) vivere così?* [Is It (Truly?!) Possible To Live This Way?], 221. Our translation.

existence, as in the words of the poet Alfieri–*I willed, always willed, very resolutely willed*–deceive me: it is a deception.[40]

So, to summarize, not just anyone or any sphere is worthy of being followed, and it is not always reasonable to trust. It is reasonable to trust and follow only if "those who expect your obedience give you reasons that correspond to the needs of your heart, those deep needs you have, the same as mine." This means that what the person tells you "could hold for all people: it is not the proposal of a sectarian concept, not attempted robbery! The person proposes values that are good for everyone and would make everyone more satisfied. Therefore the person proposes things that correspond to the depths of your heart; they are not the outcome of provisional and torturously cerebral analyses of the situation. No, no. It's a matter of fundamental things that nourish and increase the fundamental good of any person; they correspond to the needs of the human heart."[41] Therefore, as I was saying, in order to trust, you must be yourself; you must be alert in order not to be deceived.

5. How can what you see in another become yours?

Now we have the elements for facing the first of the questions raised by our friend. How can the hope she recognized in the people she met and in the place

40 *Ibid.*, p. 222.
41 *Ibid.*, p. 224.

where her heart was rekindled, become hers? How can she reasonably entrust herself to that hope?

Hope can become hers by continuing the journey she began, with ever greater awareness and desire, that is, by following the people who made hope evident for her, and for whom adequate reasons for trust emerged. Following is the road.

Together with the word "follow" we can also use the word "responsibility," in the sense of Peter's immediate response to Jesus's question, "Simon, do you love Me?". "Yes."[42] It was a *yes* that not even his betrayal a few days before could restrain, because it was born as the consequence of the wonder that began with his first encounter with that man, an attachment that intensified in the years of shared living with Him and that was not a sentimental phenomenon, but rather one of reason, a judgement that glued him to that presence that had looked at him, embraced and loved him like no one else in his life. "If I am because I am loved, I have to respond (*respondeo*): this is the origin of 'responsibility' […] It is the word 'responsibility' that assures the outcome of an experience of correspondence with the truth, with the fascination of beauty, with the moving experience of the good, with ineffable happiness." This responsibility "is expressed as freedom's decision in front of the Presence that is acknowledged as corresponding totally to one's destiny."[43]

Often our way of understanding the decision of freedom is ambiguous, as if it were a matter of will,

---

[42] Cf. Jn 21:15-17.
[43] L. Giussani-S. Alberto-J. Prades, *Generating Traces in the History of the World*, 65-69.

a synonym of "willpower." Instead, as it was for Simon Peter, it is the emergence of esteem and affection, the culmination of attachment. In order for the hope we have seen in others who fascinated and attracted us to become our own, we need just the simplicity to remain attached to this place, submerged in this companionship of ours. Over time we will discover in ourselves an indestructible positiveness, together with the boldness to challenge the future.

But here a verification is especially important, in freedom. This companionship, this place is a space of freedom where each person is encouraged to carry out the verification of the promise received. It would not be a Christian companionship if it did not encourage personal verification and if it did not love freedom. A young woman who met a community of university students told me, "I understood that this was my place, because freedom is respected. They don't pressure me to do anything. They wait for something to happen in me and for me to yield to it." This is the sign of the Mystery's scrupulous respect for our freedom, having created us free. You can break off from this companionship at any time, but it remains, and this is the greatest gesture of friendship toward those who for various reasons leave: there is a place where you can always return.

"Dearest Fr. Julián, I recently registered for the Spiritual Exercises of the Fraternity, after twelve years! I participated in my last Exercises in 2009 with my heart vacillating because of an uncertain judgment about the value of my journey in the Movement. In fact, after years of sincere presence in the Movement, I realized I was trapped in formalism and activism. I did things for the Movement, many in fact, but they weren't for me anymore. My freedom wasn't there anymore, and maybe not even my faith. So I decided to leave everything. In December of that same year when I came to you to deliver my 'no,' your answer surprised me: an embrace that I've carried with me and that has kept me company, until I could return to say, twelve years later, 'Here I am. I'm here. I want to be here!'. You told me, 'Go. Don't worry about leaving a form, but take care never to forget the question of every morning: 'Where is my hope based today?'. Since then I've lived for years entirely dedicated to work as a physician, which led me to a hospital department head who I knew only through his scientific publications, in an unknown city. From our first phone call, he struck and fascinated me, but only when I began working for him did I understand what was behind that fascination: he was a man of faith, and a member of the Movement, no less! What can I say? Jesus played 'a great trick' on me, or better, gave me a wonderful gift that I experienced and experience as the sign of His love for me and of His forgiveness. He gave me the chance to resume the road I had left, making me find it again in the daily life, difficult and at times dry, of my work. So with time I started doing School of Community again, and a few days ago I registered for the Spiritual Exercises, certain of my need to participate in them. From my experience I can say that hope exists; it is unconditional and poses no limits (my fragility was no limit). It lives in a Presence and 'only' needs to be desired, every day."

The journey of verification is necessary for everyone, concerns everyone, every day, in every phase of life, as circumstances succeed each other and change, until the end.

"I asked to become a member in the Fraternity just a year ago. I had abandoned the Movement thirty years before, at the end of my university studies because my days were full of activities and relationships but the meaning of everything was lost and taken for granted, so life was arid [if our companionship is not a journey to destiny, life becomes arid and then this companionship does not interest us any more]. These thirty years have been beautiful and full of the simple and beautiful events of family, children and work, as it is for most people. Then three years ago I discovered I was ill and so my life changed and accelerated, and with this also my entreaty for meaning. I happened to meet a physician who is in the Movement and I asked him for help. He invited me to the Beginning Day and I remember very well my great wonder at discovering an unexpected correspondence with the words. I felt they described and understood my heart and the essential nature of what I desire. After so many years of distance, it's stunning to find correspondence in this very place. I never would have believed it possible! A very simple but meaningful and radical friendship began with some people and even in these months of pandemic when we rarely met, this relationship has been the most important point of reference for me. This friendship communicates the precious possibility of a road that is a good hypothesis for my life, something I've never found elsewhere. Last December I went to the hospital for periodic tests and as I was waiting for the results I realized with wonder that I wasn't afraid. This certainly was not the fruit of persuasion, lines of reasoning or willpower. It's evident to me that the experience of these two years, the gestures in which I participated, the few moments of friendship I was able to share have slowly but surely built the certainty that reality is positive because of the presence of an Other. The beauty of many moments, the wonder and gratitude for having encountered a place where I can talk about my truest questions have opened a breach in me and built me up in a way I was almost unaware of. Hope is not something to be achieved; it is not attained on the basis of circumstances that have to occur in a certain way, for example, through my definitive healing from this illness or the end of the pandemic. Hope is already here, working in my life and even influencing my experience of illness. It has become a concrete and undeniable experience of the possibility of the hundredfold on earth here and now."

In order to reach certainty about the presence of Christ and to live as ours the hope this place communicates to us, we need to carry out a personal verification in which we examine more deeply the evidence of the beginning so it may become conviction. What we have encountered does not become our through magic or sentimentalism, but through a trajectory of experience that confirms the initial intuition. As we have said, this is the dynamic that the apostles experienced. "And His disciples began to believe in Him."[44] This expression marked the steps of their journey, and the same holds for us: everything that happens in our days can become the opportunity for this verification and confirmation. Nothing should be censured along

[44] Jn 2:11; see here, p. 99.

the journey. Rather, this is the one way to reach certainty about the promise we have received: comparing ourselves with everything that happens.

"These weeks of university election campaigning have been very full, with very beautiful days. Even though I was cooped up at home and physically alone in front of a computer, I experienced a concrete happiness and discovered more about who I am and the value of relationships. But after those beautiful days and with the end of the elections I felt invaded by despondency and a huge sense of judgment of myself: I perceived my inability not to be determined by the outcome. The beauty of those weeks did not hold up in front of the sadness determining me, and at the same time I feared losing the beauty I'd experienced, erasing it or retaining just the feeling of defeat. The days after the vote made a lot of uncomfortable questions emerge in me and they gave me no peace. Why wasn't the happiness of the previous weeks enough? What holds up against the disappointment of the result? Why do I tend to erase the beauty I experienced? I wasn't elected, so what's there for me? The dissatisfaction and sadness initially led me to close myself off from others and my parents, with whom I live. And yet, after a couple of days my need to judge those weeks and not lose them got the upper hand. This led me to ask help from my friends, in particular to talk about the most uncomfortable part, the way I felt scandalized by my own reactions. It unleashed a struggle between my own measure of myself and of what I do, of the sadness I feel, and the happiness I experienced and would like to experience forever. A friend pointed out how this circumstance exalted my humanity, and this shook me up because I didn't see anything positive in my being scandalized at my own reactions. Instead, on the one hand, I see my human smallness that I can no longer avoid looking at, and on the other hand, the fact that I was happy simply to give myself, to communicate to others what I live."

In order not to get stymied in our personal verification, we need to be inside a companionship that constantly breaks our measure and reopens our eyes, allowing us to see what we would otherwise miss.

It is instructive to consider the way Jesus challenged Peter's measure day after day. An exemplary scene is when He washed the disciples' feet. "During supper, fully aware that the Father had put everything into His power and that He had come from God and was returning to God, He rose from supper and took off His outer garments. He took a towel and tied it around His waist. Then He poured water into a basin and began to wash the disciples' feet and dry them with the towel around His waist. He came to Simon Peter, who said to Him, 'Master, are you going to wash my feet?' Jesus answered and said to him, 'What I am doing, you do not understand now, but you will understand later'." When Peter responded, "You will never wash my feet!", Jesus raiseed the stakes, radicalizing the challenge. "Unless I wash you [your feet], you will have no inheritance with Me." Peter yielded. "Master, [if You put it this way] then not only my feet, but my hands and head as well."[45] What won out in him, causing his sudden about-face, inducing him not to let his own measure prevail? His affection for Christ.

[45] Jn 13:3-9.

In order not be imprisoned in our own frameworks, which inexorably form in us and we draw from the surrounding environment, we must be regenerated continuously. "A judgment permanently open and without prejudices is, in fact, impossible for purely human efforts, but it is the only one that respects and exalts the dynamism of reason (which is openness to reality according to all its factors)."[46] In order for this to be possible, we need a place that continually throws our reason wide open again, over and over; this place is "a particular that renders one capable of the whole,"[47] as Giussani defined the experience of the charism. Therefore, in order not to succumb to the measures that inevitably tend to rigidify our judgement and upon which we often get stranded, neither a titanic effort nor a shrewd strategy are needed. It is necessary simply not to stop looking at the living reality that sustains the broadening of our reason; we need affection for the place that enables us to see the totality, not allowing the original openness of reason to diminish.

The more we experience how this place can regenerate our gaze on ourselves and the world, the more our affection for it will grow. The verification deepens, nourishes and substantiates the awareness of belonging to the instrument that Christ has chosen to attract and accompany our life.

This is exactly the same dynamic of the beginning, when the disciples lived in companionship with Jesus.

---

[46] L. Giussani-S. Alberto-J. Prades, *Generating Traces in the History of the World*, 54.
[47] *Ibid.*, 80.

Each day they spent with Him, Giussani said with a beautiful expression, added another "coat of glue,"[48] deepened their attachment, which was a judgment of esteem, full of reasons, without even a shadow of irrationality or forcing. At the same time, if we carry out a verification of the proposal made by the companionship we have encountered, our immanence in this companionship will make us ever more reasonably attached to it and above all will introduce us to the increasingly personal discovery of the Presence of which it is a sign and visible face: Christ, our hope. In fact, this is the purpose for which the companionship exists. Therefore, what happened to the disciples happens to us today as well: from the attachment to His presence arises the flower of hope.

In the last book of the Spiritual Exercises of the Fraternity, just published, Giussani said, "Peter had done just about all the wrong he could do, yet he lived a supreme sympathy for Christ. He understood that everything in him tended to Christ, that everything was gathered in those eyes, in that face, in that heart. His past sins could not amount to an objection, nor even the incoherence he could imagine for the future. Christ was the source, the place of his hope. Had someone objected to what he had done or what he might have done, Christ remained, through the gloom of those objections, the source of light for his hope. And he esteemed Him above everything else, from the first moment in which he had felt himself stared at by His eyes, looked on by Him. This is why

[48] *Ibid.*, 69.

he loved Him. 'Yes, Lord, you know You are the object of my supreme sympathy, of my highest esteem'."[49]

Christ is the source of light of our hope, and the companionship formed through the grace of the charism gifted to Fr. Giussani is a help to live our conversion to Christ, "because the essence of the experience of the Movement is that faith is everything, the acknowledgment of Christ is everything in life, that Christ is the center of the cosmos and history."[50] The fraternity among us, the warp and weft of relationships that constitute the Movement "is our way of living the mystery of Christ present".[51] It is not an easy escape from living the personal drama of the relationship with Christ. On the contrary, it is a help and a provocation to live it more intensely and consciously. I want to live constantly the drama of my freedom that drives me to say 'You' to Christ as soon as I open my eyes in the morning. Jesus Himself lived this same drama. "Rising very early before dawn, He left and went off to a deserted place, where He prayed."[52] This is the level where we stake our lives. "The moment has come," Giussani said exactly thirty years ago, "when the Movement must walk exclusively in force of the affection for Christ each of us has, each of us invokes

[49] L. Giussani, *Attraverso la compagnia dei credenti* [Through the Companionship of the Believers], 132. This text covering Giussani's writings 1994-1996 is only available in Italian at the moment. The English translation of this passage is quoted in *Generating Traces in the History of the World*, 61.
[50] L. Giussani, *Una strana compagnia* [A Strange Companionship], 191-192. Our translation.
[51] L. Giussani, *The Work of the Movement. The Fraternity of Communion and Liberation,* trans. Susan Scott (Milan: Cooperativa Editoriale Nuovo Mondo, 2005), 71.
[52] Mk 1:35.

the Holy Spirit for."[53] Therefore, the Movement continues in force of the affection of each of us for Christ. All the rest–our efforts, our intentions–is too fragile.

So, not only does this fabric of relationships not spare us the relationship with the Mystery, but it incessantly prompts us to this relationship and constantly makes it possible. In fact, if the Mystery did not make itself present now through a human companionship, a place, a fabric of relationships, it would remain extraneous and we would be dominated by the common mentality, which lives on hopes that do not bear up to the impact of events, and which tries in many ways to expunge the Mystery from life.

It is precisely the Mystery present that we all need for living. "People, young and no longer young, need only one thing: the certainty that their time and life are positive, the certainty of their destiny."[54] But this certainty, which is called "hope," is not something we can give ourselves, not even if we coalesce together, work in solidarity, and converge all our efforts. Only God made man, with His death and resurrection, can respond to the thirst for destiny, for existence to be positive, which structures us from within. As we have said, the encounter with His presence in the form that attracted us is the grace of our life, the infinite compassion of the Lord for our nothingness, but we cannot keep it for ourselves as if it were a privilege.

---

[53] "Corresponsibilità". Stralci dalla discussione al Consiglio internazionale di CL–agosto 1991 ["Co-responsibility." Excerpts from the discussion of the International Council of CL, August 1991], *Tracce-Litterae communionis,* n. 11/1991. Our translation.

[54] Cf. L. Giussani, "Christ, the hope", *CL Litterae Communionis,* n. 11/1990, p. 6. Our translation.

"I was at the university studying when a classmate I hadn't seen for months stopped by to say hello. She began telling me about herself, her paralyzing fear about the pandemic situation, her hope based on the fact that science would take its course and the vaccine would bring us back to normalcy. She said until then she would be condemned to suspension of her life. I told her that for me, circumstances are a factor of my maturation and I recounted with wonder that the biggest grace was to have faces and a place where I can return to beg for a truer gaze on myself. A few days later she wrote to thank me, saying it had been years since she'd had a conversation 'with so much sense.' Her heart desires what I desire: certainty in the present with which to meet everything fearlessly. In these months from the lockdown onwards, I have felt loved just as I am, full of gratitude for having in front of me people who, through the way they live and look at themselves with sincerity, generate in me hope for my life. Recognizing Christ present in my day has become more continual and generates an upwelling of emotion that puts my heart in an ever truer position in front of everything. I discover the truth of what was written on the Christmas poster. 'The presence of Christ, in the ordinariness of life, increasingly involves the beat of our heart: being moved by His presence turns into being moved in our daily lives. Nothing is useless; nothing is extraneous.We start to have an affection for everything, *everything*'."

Christ, as a real event today and not simply a real event two thousand years ago, enters into the normalcy of living and transforms it, making it truer, more human. If Christ is a real event for me, if I accept Him and let Him enter into the warp and weft of my days, this is documented in a change that takes place in my life. "Christianity," said Fr. Giussani in 1964, "is a new way to live in this world. It is a new life. Above all, it does not represent a few particular experiences, ways of doing things, additional gestures, or expressions or words to add to our usual vocabulary." He continued, "Today, the Christian proposal, like the encounter, is identified with the call to us from a human reality surrounding us; and it is magnificent that this unique proposal among all others should have such a concrete, existential face, that it should be a community in the world, a world in the world, a different reality within reality; and not different because it has different interests but because of the different way in which it pursues commone interests."[55]

When people come up against the event of Christ and embrace it, they are different, and this difference communicates hope.

But we cannot stop here even for a moment. The attraction we experience through the renewal of the encounter and immanence in the Christian companionship must become a work, a vigilance in us ("like someone who has conquered something beautiful and must defend it, and therefore is up on the ramparts and does not sleep, is not distracted or superficial, is alert"); it must become memory, and memory "is not remembering, but a continual conformation to a presence that, once it revealed itself, did so as presence that does not leave; once it is revealed to *us*, it is

55 L. Giussani, *The Journey to Truth is an Experience*, trans. John Zucchi, McGill-Queen's University Press, Montreal, 2006, pp. 94, 97.

revealed as a presence that does not leave (because it constitutes us) and makes itself perceivable, visible in others, a presence that puts us together with the goal of being lived. In fact, it is called communion, exactly like the Eucharist."[56]

[56] L. Giussani, *"Tu" (o dell'amicizia)* ["You" or On Friendship], Bur, Milano 1997, pp. 318, 319. Our translation.

CHAPTER 6

HOPE PUT TO THE TEST BY CIRCUMSTANCES

"Those who follow Me will receive a hundred times more now in this present age."[1] Jesus Himself gave a criterion for the verification of life following in His footsteps. In the same way, the hope promised to those who follow Him must–I insist–be verified in the comparison with circumstances, none excluded.

1. Hope that does not disappoint

The hope that does not disappoint promised by Christ must demonstrate that it holds up in the face of the challenges that human existence is forced to face and that these times have set before everyone's eyes mercilessly. Like it or not, everyone is called to verify the substance of their hope in front of every problematic situation, every provocation, the most meaningful ones in particular. We said with Giussani that "people, young and no longer young, ultimately need one thing: the certainty that their time and life are positive, certainty about their destiny." In front of certain circumstances, it comes to light whether we have this certainty, or whether fear and uncertainty prevail and

[1] Cf. Mk 10:29-30.

block constructiveness, causing us to crumble into worry and making us stay centered on ourselves.

Therefore, the fundamental contribution for a verification of our hope comes from reality. Circumstances are crucial so that, on the one hand, the substance of our hope is manifested, and on the other hand, true hope becomes rooted in our innermost depths. Therefore, to verify whether Christian hope does not disappoint, we must face the things reality does not spare us, in the encounter and in the clash with circumstances, especially the inevitable ones. The hope that has been communicated and witnessed to us makes its dwelling place in us and becomes ours "only" in the relationship with circumstances along the journey through a verification.

a) Death

Let us consider first the greatest stumbling block, which from a certain point of view comes last, inasmuch as it happens at the end of our life, but that accompanies every moment of our lives as an uncomfortable and unnerving inhabitant of human consciousness: death. How can we have certainty in the future without facing the fiercest adversary? The great historian Huizinga wrote that death is part of a definition of life. "In history, as in nature, the processes of death and birth are eternally in step with one another."[2] Death is a phenomenon of life, because it happens

---

[2] J. Huizinga, *The Autumn of the Middle Ages*, trans. Rodne J. Payton and Ulrich Mammitzsch (Chicago: The University of Chicago Press, 1996), XIX.

to a living being, and thus it is a problem that cannot be eluded, much less by a being that is conscious of itself, as we are. The knowledge of death characterizes in an essential way the consciousness we have of ourselves, even if we try to censure it in many ways. The pandemic has restored to the foreground for everyone the elementary evidence of death. It may not have been so familiar to us in the past, and in our daily life we may have forgotten and covered it, but now we have been forced to acknowledge it, not like someone observing it from the balcony or on television, but as those who have been touched by it and forced to deal with it. All of us could experience this because death came close as family members or friends passed away and because every day we had to and still have to deal with the number of deaths. We are all challenged, and nobody can pretend that reality is less "somber and dark."

Let's see together how Giussani perceived the challenge of death. Reading the breviary, he paused on a line in the book of *Wisdom*, "For God did not make Death, He takes no pleasure in destroying the living. To exist–for this He has created all things; the creatures of the world have health in them, in them is no fatal poison, and Hades has no power over the world: for uprightness is immortal. (Wis 1:13-15, *The New Jerusalem Bible*)." And he observed during a meeting in 1990, "I was struck by a deep rebellion. I cried, because those words were not true. It is not true that justice reigns immortal in a world in which two of our friends, Marco and Andrea, can die on a hike in the mountains. And yet," he added immediately, "without adhering in some way to this expression you could not live; without a positive hope you could not live." Now, he continued, in order to agree with this expression, people have two alternatives. "The first is optimism–which is instinctive inasmuch as it is necessary–without a foundation. This is the optimism that dominates modern culture, the roots of which have been the same all throughout the ages. Indeed, we have inherited it from the Greek and Roman world. It is an optimism that considers a superficial lie. Whoever pretends to maintain this optimism would have to be deeply distracted from that which happens near him. The second possibility is the reaction with the strength of our will, with our own constructive capacity. This, too, is a characteristic of our world. We place life's solution in utopias, in the construction of our own projects. We fix our gaze on a dream and thus on a limited and particular hope. Every form of utopia (from women to money or politics), as an answer to the thirst for positivity that comes from within the heart of Man, implies violence."[3]

Thus these are the alternatives, full of lies and misunderstanding, both of them insufficient.

It is true that we are made for life. The passage in *Wisdom* affirms the nature of the human heart, but who will give an answer to this nature of the heart, to our irrepressible and constitutive desire for life? It is Christ, only Christ dead and risen, who gives an answer. "The only response possible for the passage from *Wisdom* is that the Word became flesh." There is no other response than that of Christ. In fact, without Christ "we would be obliged to fall into an optimism

[3] L. Giussani, "Christ, the hope," *CL Litterae Communionis*, 3.

that is phony, presumptuous and cynical even when it is offered by great philosophers, or into banal and grandiose utopianism, in any case full of violence."[4]

The line from *Wisdom* touches the center of the human question; from the point of view of the human heart it is the most delicate and important issue. God "fashioned all things that they might have being, and the creatures of the world are wholesome; there is not a destructive drug among them nor any domain of Hades on earth, for righteousness is undying." Giussani insisted at a point shortly before the one quoted here, that without Christ "this would not be true, because the contradiction ends up destroying everything you have imagined and built, and sucking it into the vortex of death. You cannot accept the truth of these words in the Bible without Christ."[5]

The dead and risen Christ is the only response to the question of *Wisdom*, that is, to the human question. As Jesus said to Nicodemus, "For God so loved the world that He gave His only Son, so that everyone who believes in Him might not perish but might have eternal life."[6] Here we find the ultimate reason and the true hope for our living: Jesus Christ here and now, a real event in the life of the human person. But all this must–I repeat–become personal experience.

A university student wrote me, "In order to answer the question 'is there hope?' I inevitably thought of a precise moment in my life, the funeral three years

---

[4] *Ibid.*, p. 15.
[5] L. Giussani, *Un evento reale nella vita dell'uomo* [A Real Event in the Life of Man] *(1990-1991)* (Milan: Bur, 2013), 149. Our translation.
[6] Jn 3:16.

ago of a friend who took her own life. In particular, when I was at the funeral, two things made me think. The first was my position at church during Mass: I spent the whole time on my knees, praying that this painful and dramatic moment could also be saved and placed in the hands of Someone greater than my own small-mindedness. The second was what happened after leaving Mass, when I was smoking a cigarette with my friends. At a certain point one turned to me and said, 'Why aren't you crying? Why aren't you in despair like us? How dare you?! It's like you're at peace.' I was a bit confused but amazed by what was happening to me. In that moment I didn't know how to describe or explain why I was that way, but I had to admit that even though I was very sad, I wasn't in despair. That suicide wasn't the last word on my life and in my heart, because even in that moment, 'something else' prevailed in me and made me seem glad. My heart was not in despair but was asking that everything of me and my friend be saved. In the midst of that pain overflowing in us, I experienced being entirely embraced! A grace that the others recognized in me! That episode changed me in the following weeks. Returning to my daily life with its little crosses and difficulties, that fact accompanied me. What a grace it is that even in front of the most dramatic and painful situations of my life, I can say there is hope! I did not invent it for myself, and it wasn't a psychological change. This hope came into my life through a living and carnal presence that took hold of me all the way to my innermost depths and changed my life. What a grace to realize this! This peace envelopes me and doesn't leave me, even in front of friends who've decided to say no to this life. Everything began with my first encounter with CL and Christianity at the university, with faces who loved me unconditionally from the very first moment, without looking at my evil, period. Precisely because of what's happened to me, and for nothing less, I could *never ever* think that my life was not valuable or lacked meaning."

Because of what has happened to her, our friend can say that she is full of "hope [that] does not disappoint,"[7] sharing the words of Saint Paul. This is the hope she experienced at the funeral: "never ever!" The ability to stay in front of and within any situation is proof that you have a hope that does not disappoint. Saint Paul wrote, "What will separate us from the love of Christ? Will anguish, or distress, or persecution, or famine, or nakedness, or peril, or the sword? [...] No, in all these things we conquer overwhelmingly through Him who loved us. For I am convinced that neither death, nor life, nor angels, nor principalities, nor present things, nor future things, nor powers, nor height, nor depth, nor any other creature will be able to separate us from the love of God in Christ Jesus our Lord."[8]

What experience do you need to have in order to say these words with certainty? It is the experience that began two thousand years ago. Let's think of John, Andrew and Peter. Once that man entered their lives, everything they did, all their affections, all their daily tasks, were connected with Him. When they followed Him, in the places He went,

[7] Rom 5:5.
[8] Rom 8:35-39.

there was no space for anything else in their hearts.[9] They saw Him on the cross and then risen. Let's imagine how they must have felt at the death of their mother or a loved one. All the concreteness of their human pain and tears remained, according to their temperaments, but there was something invincible in them, a gladness, because they had in their eyes that Man, dead and risen. This affected forever how they looked at everything. As Pope Francis said, "It is the companionship of a Presence that does not depend in the final analysis on external circumstances, but is given; a familiarity with Jesus in which you progress day after day."[10]

Giussani witnessed this to us until the end of his life. At the end of the 2004 Spiritual Exercises of the Fraternity, in what would be his last greeting, in a situation of evident limitation and suffering, he said, "Christ's victory is a victory over death. And the victory over death is a victory over life. Everything has a positivity, everything is a good […] so much so that any contradiction or any pain has, in the 'vehicle' of this life, a positive answer. […] Because life is beautiful: life is beautiful; it is a promise God made with the victory of Christ. Therefore, every day that we get out of bed–whatever our immediately perceptible, documentable situation may be, even the most

[9] Cfr. L. Giussani, *Si può (veramente?!) vivere così?* [Is It (Truly?!) Possible to Live This Way?], 363-364. Our translation.
[10] Pope Francis, *Il Cielo sulla Terra* [Heaven on Earth] (Vatican City: LEV, 2020), 272. Our translation.

painful, unimaginable–is a good that is about to be born on the edge of our horizon as men."[11]

This irreducible positivity even in the face of death is proof that you have a hope that does not disappoint, a hope that is the experience of something that exists. "The future is grounded on something we possess now, by which we are possessed now."[12]

b) Suffering

Like death, suffering is also part of human life, not only the suffering related to our own finitude itself, but also that provoked by the responsibility of women and men. "We must do all we can to overcome suffering, but to banish it from the world altogether is not in our power. This is simply because we are unable to shake off our finitude and because none of us is capable of eliminating the power of evil, of sin which, as we plainly see, is a constant source of suffering."[13] The way we deal with suffering itself and those who suffer is an indicator of the truth of the human experience of each of us and of society as a whole. In our contexts of life we see a growing censure of suffering, an increasing tendency to flee from everything that could require suffering or participation in the affliction of

[11] L. Giussani, "Closing Words from Fr. Giussani," in *The Destiny of Man,* 2004 Spiritual Exercises of the Fraternity of Communion and Liberation, 48, available at https://english.clonline.org/pubblications/other-texts/fraternity-exercises

[12] L. Giussani, *Tutta la terra desidera il Tuo volto* [All the Earth Desires Your Face] (Cinisello Balsamo (Mi): San Paolo, 2015), 56. Our translation.

[13] Benedict XVI, Encyclical letter *Spe salvi*, 36.

others. And yet we see that there is no true relationship with others without sharing their suffering; there cannot be a loving relationship without expropriation of self. You do not affirm goodness, truth and justice without accepting the suffering that this entails (and when protection of your own well-being becomes more important than truth and justice, the power of the most powerful, intimidation and deceit dominate). The same holds for personal suffering: no matter how much we try to elude it, in the final analysis it is never avoidable. It would be like avoiding life itself. When truly grave trials put our backs to the wall, we realize that our little or big hopes, our optimistic thoughts or projects are insufficient for facing them. "The certitude of that true, great hope"[14] becomes necessary, the certainty of a Presence that can embrace our drama.

As Pope Francis wrote in *Lumen fidei*: "To those who suffer, God does not provide arguments which explain everything; rather, His response is that of an accompanying presence, a history of goodness which touches every story of suffering and opens up a ray of light. In Christ, God Himself wishes to share this path with us and to offer us His gaze so that we might see the light within it. Christ is the one who, having endured suffering, is 'the pioneer and perfector of our faith' (*Heb* 12:2). Suffering reminds us that faith's service to the common good is always one of hope."[15]

Our essential need is to see witnesses to this great, true hope born of faith, people whose lives demonstrate that in Christ's company and Presence you can

[14] *Ibid.*, 39.
[15] Francis, Encyclical letter *Lumen fidei*, 57.

live suffering without sinking into the darkness of solitude, of the void of meaning, of abandonment. As Benedict XVI wrote, with Christ and His death and resurrection, "in all human suffering we are joined by one who experiences and carries that suffering *with* us; hence *con-solatio* is present in all suffering, the consolation of God's compassionate love–and so the star of hope rises."[16] This is what witnesses show us. "Because it has now become a shared suffering, though, in which another person is present, this suffering is penetrated by the light of love."[17] Suffering that is not shared and embraced by a Presence who never leaves, by the love of God through the love of women and men, becomes blind and unbearable.

"In November 2019 I was diagnosed with a very aggressive, advanced stage cancer. In the beginning the shock overwhelmed me and my family. I felt at the mercy of adverse and totally uncontrollable events. Everything began to change when a friend came to visit and told me that I shouldn't feel tossed about in that condition, but rather, embraced by Christ. From that time on, I began to put myself in His arms and entrust myself to the design of an Other. Everything I had listened to, read and repeated for many years suddenly became flesh. My faith was in play and I was asked to pass 'from theory to practice.' I accepted the challenge of verifying the hypothesis offered me, that Christ had not abandoned me and was with me in that circumstance. The fruits of grace were not slow to arrive. My relationships with my husband and

---

[16] Benedict XVI, Encyclical letter *Spe salvi*, 39.
[17] *Ibid.*, 38.

children began to change; I started looking at them as the nearest form of Christ's companionship in my life. Even the physical and most acute pain that frightens us and shows all our fragility was not an obstacle. I began to love the circumstances, to wake up in the morning embracing the day with the enthusiasm of a child expecting a deeply desired gift from her parents. The relationship with old and new friends became precious and was renewed. What seemed like an extinguished friendship instead proved that it is a companionship for life, bringing the same intensity to bear on the important things and the smallest needs. I was hospitalized for a long time, and encounters happened and new relationships were forged with physicians, nurses and roommates. It would be hard to tell about the many encounters that happened, but one in particular marked me considerably. I had to undergo a second operation and though usually I'm optimistic by nature, I was afraid and didn't feel able to face it. The evening before the operation a friend I'd met because of the cancer kept me company, and at the end of our conversation, he asked me what 'living reality intensely' meant for me in that moment. With the experience I'd had up to then in my heart, I spontaneously told him that it meant enjoying everything, even those moments, but to do so it was necessary to go to the origin of each thing, continuing to acknowledge the presence of Christ in reality and my life. He encouraged me to remember this desire as the last thought before the operation and as soon as I woke up afterwards. The surgery left me dazed and the doctors informed me right away that I would have to stay immobile in bed for ten days. I asked myself how I could live intensely, given that the anesthesia and pain confused my perception of reality and I wasn't allowed to move. What did meeting Christ mean for me, unable to do anything except turn my head in bed? In that moment, I realized that turning my head, notwithstanding the confusion, reality existed, and I began looking. I saw the walls of the room in front of me and above all that there was another person in the room with me, but the night stand blocked my view and I could only see her legs. This new roommate had my same name and suffered the same type of tumor. We began telling each other about our lives, and in the long month we spent together we told each other everything. Taking advantage of the hospitalization, I asked to receive Communion every day, and my friend initially watched with curiosity, asking me many questions. One morning she asked to receive Communion too, and with the chaplain, the 'little monk' as we called him, we began to pray together. As the days passed our room became a place where we asked ourselves what was essential in life. This level of relationship between us involved whoever entered the room, doctors, nurses, social workers, cleaning staff, and relatives and friends who came to visit. Even my husband and friend did not come to visit just for me, but also for her. Our room became a place where all sorts of things happened. Its walls had 'expanded' and it attracted everyone. I asked my husband to bring me *Traces* and an extra copy for my friend, and she read it with curiosity, especially the letters, and never stopped talking about Cardinal Van Thuan. When she learned that he was buried in Rome, she told me she deeply desired to go to his grave. One day, after reading the CAT scan report, she understood the true gravity of her situation. I asked, not only for her, but above all for me, 'Where do I place my hope? In healing? Or in the certainty that everything is truly for the good, even pain or death, and that He who loved and loves me in every instant is there, He who made me for eternity and not dissolution in oblivion?' Then the hope I could bring her was quite different from the optimism of those who want to close their eyes. We left the hospital only a few days apart and the relationship with my ex-roommate continued intensely even though we lived in different cities. In the beginning, things seemed to go well but after a few weeks I understood she was getting worse and worse. She wrote me that she felt the disease progressing quickly and her strength diminishing, that she was tired and the doctors couldn't do anything more for her. I was filled with pain, and tried to tell her I continued praying, even for a miracle. I wanted to do something for her but I felt powerless. While I was absorbed in these thoughts, I didn't realize that she had written me the one reasonable thing: she wanted to abandon herself in the arms of the Lord. My husband pointed it out to me. 'But look, she's at peace!' I decided to go visit her in her home, and my husband and friend accompanied me. She was very badly off, and confessed that what she desired more than anything else was to be able to receive Communion. When we left her home, we looked for the closest church and the priest there said he would go the next day for Confession, Communion and Annointing of the Sick. Two days later she died. In the following days I wrote her partner, telling him I was grateful for having met her and was certain that she died 'in the grace of God' and in peace. He answered that in the last moments she was unconscious, but before dying she'd opened her eyes, smiled, and then went in peace. What happened is surprising. It's amazing that through a small willingness to stay in reality, all this could happen! Christ made Himself present even in the apparently hostile circumstance of being confined to bed and unable to do anything more than turn my head."

c) Evil

How common it is to be or feel a prisoner of your errors, gripped by the alternative between demoralization for having erred, complaint for not having been up to the challenge, and perennial justification of yourself, dumping responsibility on others and on situations. We oscillate between desperation and presumption, where the second comes to interrupt and take over from the first. And with every error of a certain significance, everything starts all over again. How easy it is to remain tangled up in your own remorse and regrets! Like Milosz' character Miguel Mañara, who lived crushed by shame for the evil he had committed. "I didn't work. [...] I lied. [...] I stole. [...] I killed. [...] I'm ashamed." But, we think often, when we see the same errors and falls repeated day after day, how is it possible not to despair? We need someone to come to rip us out of our condition, to free us from the grip of evil, from the measure we project on ourselves. "The fact is that you think about things that no longer exist (and that never existed, my son)," said the Abbot to Miguel Mañara, adding, "You think too much about your pain. Why do you seek pain? Why do you fear losing what was able to find you? Penitence is not pain. It is love." This discovery is what makes Miguel Mañara say his *yes* to the One who found him. "I am Mañara. And He who loves me tells me these things never happened! He alone is."[18]

The evil is reduced to zero by the infinite power of Christ's forgiveness. The *yes* that Milosz has the protagonist of his play speak is the echo of Simon's *yes* to Jesus, "pronounced through his awareness of the forgiveness in the face that asks him, 'Simon, do you love Me?' [...] The *yes* of Saint Peter is built upon this forgiveness."[19] Therefore, with all that we realistically know of ourselves, with all our capacity for evil and error, we can hope, we can get up again, because the relationship that the Mystery made flesh, Christ present here and now, established with us is dominated by forgiveness, *is* forgiveness. Grounded in this forgiveness, we start over again a thousand times a day. Only in forgiveness is our life born again, only in forgiveness is there construction.

"Everyone who has this hope based on Him makes Himself pure, as He is pure,"[20] said Saint John in his first Letter, and Giussani commented, in a thrilling passage, "Our hope is in Christ, in that Presence that, however distracted and forgetful we be, we can no longer (not completely anyway) remove from the earth

[18] O.V. Milosz, *Miguel Mañara*, *Mefiboseth*, *Saulo di Tarso* (Milan: Jaca Book, 2010), 47-49, 52, 63. Our translation from the Italian translation.
[19] L. Giussani, *Attraverso la compagnia dei credenti* [Through the Companionship of the Believers], 155-156. Our translation.
[20] 1 Jn 3:3.

of our heart because of the tradition through which He has reached us. It is in Him that I hope, before counting my errors and my virtues. Numbers have nothing to do with this. In the relationship with Him, numbers don't count, the weight that is measured or measurable is irrelevant, and all the evil I can possibly do in the future has no relevance either. It cannot usurp the first place that this *yes* of Simon, repeated by me has before the eyes of Christ. So a kind of flood comes from the depths of our heart, like a breath that rises from the breast and pervades the whole person, making it act, making it want to act more justly. The flower of the desire for justice, for true, genuine love, the desire to be capable of acting gratuitously, springs up from the depths of the heart."[21]

d) *The uncertainty of the future*

Those who have made a journey in which they have seen their own life change find they have a certainty about the future that is amazing. Tomorrow no longer has an uncertain and fear-inspiring face.

A university student wrote, "In this unexpected and overwhelming historical period, it often happens that I settle for semi-normalcy, sliding into complaints and tantrums. However, I can't help but notice deep down in myself a strange positiveness that remains, that is not uprooted even by the most difficult days. A few days ago I was studying in the library, absorbed in my

[21] L. Giussani-S. Alberto-J. Prades, *Generating Traces in the History of the World*, 61-62.

thoughts, and a younger housemate sought me out and asked, 'Do you think I'll ever be happy?' Without hesitation and with a smile I assured her yes. Later, I asked myself what made me guarantee 100% that a person would be happy? Why am I certain that there is hope? I realized that my story talks of this. Following Christ changed my life, not that I'm self-sufficient or my dramas are all resolved. To the contrary, I'm very distracted and often I let my usual old failures cloud over me. Following Christ changed my life, because after years and years of attempts and falls, of periods when I gave in to the difficulty and then returned more or less responsible, I've begun to have a growing awareness that everything is for me. The only thing that loosens my grip on what I have in mind, my projects, is the experience of continually being filled anew by Christ. I realize it right away, because it is like I begin to rest, like I return to my home after so much wandering."

Following Christ changes your life. It is the description of an experience, not a cliché. As our friend wrote, what frees her from thoughts and projects is "continually being filled anew by Christ." She realizes it right away, because of what happens in her. It is "like I begin to rest." She experiences this change in the present and it gives her certainty about the future, that is, hope that enables her to answer immediately *yes* when her younger friend asks if she'll ever be happy. Without certainty in the present, which makes it possible to look at the future with certainty, she never would have been so bold as to answer a question like that with an immediate *yes*. She would not have had the energy to sustain that yes. Instead, this becomes possible in a place that generates a "strange positiveness" in those who belong: they begin to wager on the future in force of a present reality.

The present reality of Christ is also the one source of peace. Only a presence able to respond to all our uncertainties about death, suffering, evil and the future can bring peace to our life, shifting the attention from ourselves to Him, and thus to others. Without presence, the hope that does not disappoint does not take root in us. What are You, O Christ, for us? The security of our hope.

2. Sustaining people's hope

We said before that hope is communicated by the difference seen in people who have encountered Christ. Therefore, Fr. Giussani stressed, "every day we must desire the change through which the hope penetrates the world." The first object of change is ourselves, our daily life, and "its endless horizon is the need of others, the help to give to meet others' needs."[22] God's goal is to reach everyone, but to do so He uses a peculiar method: He reaches everyone through some. This is the method chosen by the Mystery to communicate Himself to the women and men of every time. In the conversation with Testori that we quoted before, Giussani reiterated this. "It seems to me that the moment has come in which the Lord, if He wants to save His work, must renew people. He must bring forth those people, those companionships, create those movements we spoke of before. The moment has come. It's

[22] Cf. L. Giussani, "Christ, the Hope," 5-6.

like the sign of the times. Therefore, paradoxically, the moment when the crisis gets the worst is the greatest moment of hope."[23]

Christ communicates Himself to the world through the human change He brings about in the life of those who encounter Him and cling to Him. In those who allow themselves to be generated by His event, an unimaginable sensitivity to the needs of others blossoms, a passion for their destiny no matter what their situation, a desire to collaborate in their concrete human journey. As Benedict XVI said, "Being in communion with Jesus Christ draws us into His 'being for all;' it makes it our own way of being. He commits us to live for others, but only through communion with Him does it become possible truly to be there for others, for the whole. [...] 'Christ died for all, that those who live might live no longer for themselves but for Him who for their sake died' (cf. *2 Cor* 5:15). Christ died for all. To live for Him means allowing oneself to be drawn into His *being for others*."[24]

This "being for others" arises through communion with Christ, through belonging to Him in the human place where He makes it possible for us to experience Him, and it is expressed in many ways according to the concrete multiplicity of needs (like those related to work) and personal situations (abandonment, solitude and suffering), thus changing society from within.

Again, here the method of God is seen. As Benedict XVI wrote, "Christianity did not bring a message

---

[23] L. Giussani–G. Testori, *Il senso della nascita* [The Meaning of Birth], 154. Our translation.

[24] Benedict XVI, Encyclical letter *Spe salvi*, 28.

of social revolution like that of the ill-fated Spartacus, whose struggle led to so much bloodshed. Jesus was not Spartacus, He was not engaged in a fight for political liberation like Barabbas or Bar-Kochba. Jesus, who himself died on the Cross, brought something totally different: an encounter with the Lord of all lords, an encounter with the living God and thus an encounter with a hope stronger than the sufferings of slavery, a hope which therefore transformed life and the world from within."[25]

A wonderful example in this sense is Saint Paul's letter to Philemon. As you know, Paul wrote a personal note from prison to Philemon of Colossae, a man Paul himself had converted to Christianity, asking him to take back his slave Onesimus, who had run away to Rome and there met Paul, converted to Christianity and put himself at Paul's service. In observation of Roman law on slavery, Paul sent Onesimus back to his legitimate owner Philemon, entrusting to him the note. "I appeal to you for my child ... whose father I have become in my imprisonment [...]. I am sending him back to you, sending my very heart [...]. Perhaps this is why he was parted from you for a while, that you might have him back for ever, no longer as a slave but more than a slave, as a beloved brother."[26] Paul appealed to the newness that the event of Christ introduces. By law, the two were master and slave, but seized by Christ, they were one thing alone. As Paul

[25] *Ibid.,* 4.
[26] Philemon 1:10-17.

wrote to the Ephesians, "Don't you know that we are members of one another?"[27]

Paul's gesture seems insignificant compared to the enormous problem of slavery, and yet it began a deep transformation that would mark history. "Even if external structures remained unaltered, this changed society from within."[28] This method may seem too slow for us; at times we wish for one that would pass over people's freedom and modify things in one stroke from above. But God's method is the only one able to obtain a radical change that respects and engages human freedom. Benedict XVI continued, "Man, in fact, is not merely the product of economic conditions, and it is not possible to redeem him purely from the outside by creating a favourable economic environment."[29] As Adrien Candiard pointed out in his book on the letter to Philemon, the change introduced by Paul's attitude is centered entirely on freedom.[30]

The undeniable harshness of the current situation, which in many ways still holds us hostage, has para-

---

[27] Cf. Rm 12:5; Eph 4:25.

[28] Benedict XVI, Encyclical letter *Spe salvi*, 4.

[29] *Ibid.*, 21.

[30] Candiard evokes the Great Inquisitor's dialogue with Jesus in Dostoevsky's novel. "Jesus, thought the Inquisitor, had got everything wrong. He had the means for placating the unbearable torture of man struggling with his own freedom. He, who is god, could have commanded him to do this or that, force him, program him, save him from himself. [...] Jesus did not do any of this. The Inquisitor accuses Jesus, 'Instead of taking possession of men's freedom, Thou didst increase it [...]. Thou didst desire man's free love, that he should follow Thee freely, enticed and taken captive by Thee.' A. Candiard, *Sulla soglia della coscienza. La libertà del cristiano secondo Paolo* [To Philemon: Reflections on Human Freedom] (Verona: EMI, 2020), 118-119. Our translation from the Italian translation of Candiard. English translation of Dostoevsky by Constance Garnett, *The Brothers Karamazov*, Chapter 5, available at https://www.mtholyoke.edu/acad/intrel/pol116/grand.htm.

doxically made it easier to discover what we need for living, what can sustain our hope. "Life is like a voyage on the sea of history, often dark and stormy, a voyage in which we watch for the stars that indicate the route. The true stars of our life are the people who have lived good lives. They are lights of hope. Certainly, Jesus Christ is the true light, the sun that has risen above all the shadows of history. But to reach Him we also need lights close by–people who shine with His light and so guide us along our way."[31] As I noted earlier, Giussani was speaking about people who are presences. Pay attention here, because these are not people endowed with out-of-the-ordinary gifts. Rather, they are people won over by the fact of Christ, made "presence" by belonging to the Christian company. A very good example is in this letter that a young mother wrote me.

"I'd like to tell you about a mother I met this year through our school. The first days of school our five-year-old son began telling me about a new boy who'd just arrived, who kept hitting him and was very irritable. I was curious to learn who this new boy was, and found out that he was the son of a woman who'd been widowed shortly before her confinement. The idea of this mother on her own, newly arrived, prompted me to seek her out, so one day in the parking lot I watched for the new faces and I asked a woman if she was the mother of the new boy in the class. She said yes, and I invited her for lunch the next day, and decided to invite two other families of the school so she could begin to meet some people. At lunch she told us a bit of her story. Her beloved husband had died of

[31] Benedict XVI, Encyclical letter *Spe salvi*, 49.

cancer at the age of 35, and now she lived alone with her four-year-old son. I immediately felt the desire to offer her companionship, as an opportunity for me, as in this period I'm dealing with my father's illness, albeit at a distance. Right off the bat, we felt comfortable and familiar with each other, and a few days later, her gratitude for my invitation moved her to invite me in turn to her home and to seek a relationship with me. I got involved in the relationship with her for what I am, entrusting every coffee through an *Angelus*, out of the inadequacy I felt, staying in front of her atheism without ever censuring what I live and asking her to tell me about what she was going through in regard to her painful situation. One morning she called me: she had just left a medical center because during the night she'd had very strong panic attacks. During breakfast she told me she was amazed that when she felt unwell I was the first person she thought to call. She was moved, and told me she didn't understand why with me she always ended up crying and was truly herself. During this conversation she confided to me about the difficulty she was going through: she hadn't wanted children, and she found herself living alone with a small child, angry at her husband for getting cancer and leaving her alone in this life. I told her clearly I was certain her husband was still present, accompanying her, even if in another form, and that what I desired for her was that she be grateful to be alive, and return to waiting expectantly for something from her days. I asked her, 'In the morning when you get up, are you grateful for still being alive another day and for breathing? Do you still think there's something beautiful waiting for you?' She told me she'd never thought this, and that nobody had ever told her the things I was telling her (actually, they seemed very simple to me). The next week we met again for a chat and she surprised me by saying she'd told her whole family about me, how grateful she was for having met me, how she had been surprised that I'd opened the door of our home to her, and that she'd even spoken of me to her therapist. She told me, 'Remember the question you asked me about whether I was grateful for being alive? The other day, when I went to my therapist, I asked him to work on this. I told him I didn't want to work on the figure of my husband and the pain anymore, and that in these months the most interesting thing I'd been told was by new friend, speaking about gratitude and life. I repeated that I wanted to work on that, because I wanted to wait expectantly for something from my days, as you'd told me.' I was speechless. I felt I'd received a grace, bowled over and seized for the *nth* time by a story and a Presence that lives inside me."

This is the documentation of a person who is a presence in normal life, in the midst of everyday circumstances. A mother meets a mother who is suffering and closed in on her pain and rage, and she shares with her the hope that grounds her life. "What a great thing we are called (no one can withdraw himself) to live together and to realize!" said Giussani. As we continue the initial journey, we discover more and more that "Asking for the same things every day, many times a day, creates a new mentality, creates a new personality, and continuously prepares us so that nothing seems unexpected or strange, not even the death of one of our own. We can suffer but not fear. Let's help each other to extend to the world that hope which cannot remove sorrow–even God, who became man and the son of a woman, experienced sorrow–but remove, from the roots, every fear."[32]

With all the load of our limitations and weaknesses, we are made presence in the normalcy of living, only because we have been reached by the event of Christ and are open to letting ourselves be embraced by Him.

"For some years now, we've had serious economic problems for various reasons, and the Fraternity itself helped us for a period. In addition to these difficulties, I've been forced to undergo long and expensive treatments. Last week, having postponed the appointments for several months so as to postpone payment, I went to the last session and asked that the bill be prepared, because I couldn't wait any longer. I'd understood during the treatments that the doctor was far from the Church and I confess that I never tried to tell him or do anything to testify to what I live. At the end of the session, having calculated what I owed him, he sat next to me and said, 'Ma'am, I hope you'll accept what I'm about to tell you. We're fine, I don't want money from you.' I looked at him without understanding, but he continued. 'What you've given me in these two years is worth more than money.' I continued not to understand. He went on, 'You can't imagine how tiring it is to work all day long listening to people complain about everything. I always see discontent people. In this period, with your positiveness, your smile,

32 L. Giussani, "Christ, the hope," 6.

your gaze when you talked about your sick daughter, helped me to live better and to look at my family and my life in a different way, full of gratitude. You've been a witness to me that life is beautiful. I'm the one who owes you something, not the other way around.' I left with my eyes full of tears, because I'm not the way that doctor described me, not at all! He didn't see me, but Christ who looked at him through me, I'm certain. I ran home to my husband saying that a miracle had happened, with my heart full of a happiness I can't describe to you. But the miracle wasn't that he waived a debt of several thousand euros: rather, it was something much greater that I didn't even look at, something the Lord wanted to surprize me with: my change, my conversion. He is also in me, even in me, and with my life, such a disaster, I can contribute even a little to making Him truly known. Seeing Him at work in the midst of all my problems and unfaithfulness, my miserableness and total incapacity, without my doing anything other than seek Him in every thing and invoke Him every time I can, made me undersand that there is a more precious good than any other good, and that He is giving me this goodness through the Movement. It is the certainty that the Lord is truly changing me. This is what filled me with a hope and serentity I'd never experienced before. Now I can say out loud all day long, 'Your grace is better than life,' because nothing has given me greater joy. Thank you, Fr. Julián, and thanks to the Fraternity and the whole story I've encountered, because without you always showing me where to look to see Him, I'd never have recognized the miracle happening in me."

Giussani said, "We are the instrument with which Christ communicates with the world. In other words, it is in the normalcy of daily life that the humanly most magnificent impetus takes root, draws nourishment, has its source, an impetus in which people communicate themselves to others, sacrifice and become a holy thing for others, bring into the lives of others the call and presence of their destiny." We are made the instrument of the communication of Christ "in this normalcy of daily life, in this normalcy in which the consciousness of His presence and the life of the companionship act, in this emotion and in this moved emotion: it is an emotion because it is beauty, the beauty of the true, the assurance of destiny, and becomes moved emotion because it moves, moves everything." Life becomes passion, "passion for being," passion "for truth, beauty, justice, love, and happiness." An unimaginable passion for being blossoms. "This positiveness is the essential feature of the gaze and affection the follower of Christ brings to the world, [...] a positiveness without end, a positiveness like a wave that invades everything."[33]

In this regard, there is a 1961 passage from von Balthasar that is worth re-reading. Over time it has not lost its value, and perhaps it has become even more pertinent. "The Body of Christ is and becomes at the same time, and thus Paul compares it to the human body, which grows toward its full stature, testing its own energies on the matter brought to it from out-

---

[33] L. Giussani, *Un evento reale nella vita dell'uomo* [A Real Event in the Life of Man] *(1990-1991)*, 105, 107. Our translation.

side and demonstrating these powers in it. The foundation of the Church and her structure cannot grow, but certainly the sphere of life can, which is prevalently formed of laypeople. People who hold an office (and who, as members, must grow like everyone) are the custodians and gardeners of growth. Laypeople must be the growth and flowering, the only ones who are capable of convincing the world of the truth of the doctrine of Christ."[34]

[34] H.U. von Balthasar, "Il laico e la Chiesa [The Layperson and the Church]," in Id., *Sponsa Verbi* (Milan: Jaca Book, 2015), 303. Our translation.

Questions and Answers*

"At times it seems to me that reality is stained in some way: there is suffering and pain, darkness and sadness. How can I live these aspects of life as well, without censuring them? What does it mean to live them intensely, and how can living everything intensely always be the road for present certainty?"

I ask myself: do you really succeed in censuring all these dramatic aspects of life–the suffering and pain, the darkness and sadness? I cannot. Whether I like it or not, in the end, they assert themselves in my life. So then, the question is how to face these aspects of existence that in the final analysis nobody can avoid. The method implied in the question often dominates: you perceive them as obstacles for your journey and so it seems more reasonable to try not to think about them, to censure them. But there is another possibility. A crucial moment in my life was when certain givens that I could not definitively eliminate and that

---

* *On the last day of the Spiritual Exercises of the Fraternity of CL (April 16-18, 2021), the contents of which are collected in this volume, there was an assembly by videoconference, during which I answered some questions Davide Prosperi asked me, summarized from the over two thousand questions that had arrived in the course of the previous evening from all over the world.*

I perceived as obstacles, as a rip off, as a measure imposed on me (because I was incapable of removing them), became "travelling companions," opportunities to go deep down into myself, into reality and into what I had encountered: Christ. It was a fundamental discovery. From then on, from within my experience, I began to understand why it is so crucial to "live always the real intensely." Only in this way can we enter into the depths of things and experience what is at the heart of life.

Many times because of the mad fear we have, we remain at appearances. We fear risk, reason's need, what we are as "given," and so we try to "buffer" everything. But this weakens and increasingly numbs us, making us less and less capable of facing situations. I do not want this! I want to live intensely so I can become certain that being vanquishes nothingness. I cannot live my whole life with a Damocles' sword over my head, with the shadow of nothingness looming over me, almost asking forgiveness for existing. Those who want to live like this, go ahead, but I cannot manage. I cannot manage any more! This is why I said that a crucial moment in my life was when all those things that seemed like an obstacle to me became the opportunity for a relationship, to involve and commit myself, to explore deep down what I had encountered. The first outcome was an entirely new discovery of reality. Now I want to continue looking it in the face. This is the reason I invited you at the beginning of the pandemic not to hide behind this or that shield to avoid dealing with reality. Those who followed this suggestion were able to realize what they have gained, but also those who did not follow it will have been able to see what they gained, whether they have become more themselves or more discouraged. Life does not cut us any slack.

I will always be grateful to Giussani for having testified to me and communicated a true gaze on reality, without veils. It entered into my blood. Through meeting him, I was able to begin looking at certain things that blocked me before, paying attention to how he looked at them. I remember the first times I participated in the gestures of the Movement: I did not understand Italian well but I could not help but experience the repercussion of the way he faced the day, he spoke, and related with people. Even though I did not understand everything, that repercussion made me return home filled with a new gaze, one I could not give myself. I had met someone who was not afraid to look at anything, anything at all, and I felt the desire not to live anymore like I was under blackmail, with my elbow raised to ward off circumstances. I had come upon a man for whom the circumstances that I initially perceived as an obstacle, with a darkened and blurred gaze, full of fear, became the opportunity for a journey, a road, to gain certainty in life.

This is the challenge for each of us. We have verified in these times how we look at reality; we cannot cheat. The testimonies I quoted showed how some people have travelled a road that has given them certain hope. Instead, others have succumbed to fear and nothingness. It has nothing to do with intelligence or how good you are. Only one thing makes the difference: taking seriously the hypothesis that it is reasonable to follow because of the encounter you have had, and verifying it. It is not a problem of IQ or ethical coherence. It is a problem of freedom and affection for your own humanity, so you will not be crushed by nothingness. The alternative is to have stamped on your face fear or certainty, a certainty lived through grace and testified to in front of anyone, beginning with your own children, a certainty that you can live everything, absolutely everything, without excluding anything, with an ultimate positiveness. I do not want to take refuge in any hiding place. I want to know whether what I live is true or not.

"Simone Weil says that true wealth is not sought, but awaited with expectancy. How does this square with the question of the risk involved in using my talents in the relationship with Jesus, in making space for Him? You said that expectant awaiting belongs to our original makeup: we are *expectant awaiting. But if we live this intensely, doesn't it risk becoming something that keeps us from living the present fully? When is risk true and worthwhile, and when is it crazy? We get blocked because we're afraid that if we risk we will lose everything: moving to a new home or job, new places and friendships, to follow a correspondence we have glimpsed. How do you decide whether to throw yourself in headlong, or not?*

I totally agree with what Simone Weil said. We can only possess true wealth by waiting expectantly. We seek it, but finding it does not depend on us. So what is the nature of the problem? Giussani defined it in the fourth chapter of *The Religious Sense.* "Our search for the ultimate meaning of our lives is not a matter of a particular intelligence, or some special effort, or even exceptional means. Rather, finding the ultimate truth is like discovering something beautiful along one's path. One sees and recognizes it, if one is attentive. The issue, then, is this attention."[1] What people desire is so disproportionate to anything they can imagine and obtain with their own strength that the one adequate attitude is to wait expectantly, with your eyes wide open. True wealth is something you wait for expectantly, the way you wait for your beloved. You can make all sorts of efforts (getting your hair done, buying a new dress, being nice) but none of these things will produce the desired presence. It arrives like a gift, absolutely unexpectedly. It can only be awaited expectantly!

The question asked how you can reconcile this expectant awaiting as a fundamental attitude of living, and risk. We wait expectantly for something that corresponds to our desire. If you are waiting for your beloved, you can only stay there on the lookout 360° to see her when she might arrive. The risk begins when you find her. If you do not want to lose her, you must risk involvement with her. You must use your talent, namely, your own humanity, which is the most precious thing you have. Otherwise you will lose her. The same thing happens in the relationship with Christ. The day John and Andrew went to John the Baptist on the banks of the Jordan River, they could not have imagined that the thing their hearts awaited would have had the form of that face: Jesus of Nazareth. Once they had come upon Him, they could have left,

[1] L. Giussani, *The Religious Sense*, 34.

like others who had met Him before them. But no, John and Andrew risked all of themselves! Was it reasonable for them to run the risk of following Him? Is it reasonable to follow someone? It depends on whom we meet. If the person who appears on your horizon does not interest you, it does not even cross your mind to risk, but if that person captures your attention, you do not want to lose her or him and so in this case the problem becomes how to "hold tight" onto the person! In front of the attraction of a presence, the most obvious, irrepressible move is to risk and get involved.

If we are not attentive to how things happen, we turn everything upside down and then, as if it were a mental game, ask how expectant awaiting and risk can stay together, without getting to the bottom of it. The first thing to do is to look at reality. Giussani underlined this with the first premise of *The Religious Sense*: "to cultivate an entire, passionate, insistent ability to observe the real event, the fact."[2] Our journey becomes more wearisome if we waste the grace of having encountered someone like Giussani. I have no hidden manual; I do not have anything different for travelling than the instruments you also have. Let's observe our experience. When we encounter something that finally corresponds to the expectant awaiting of the heart, taking a risk is supremely worthwhile because it would be folly to miss it. Risking would not be folly. It would be folly to miss out on what immensely interests us. Risking on something of no value would be folly, because there would not be adequate reasons.

[2] *Ibid.*, 4.

In its sublime simplicity, the Gospel expresses what we have said. "The kingdom of heaven is like a treasure buried in a field, which a person finds and hides again, and out of joy goes and sells all that he has and buys that field."[3] Is it folly to risk everything to buy the field, or is it the deal of a lifetime?

Saint Paul had it very clearly. "I even consider everything as a loss because of the supreme good of knowing Christ Jesus my Lord." What had he encountered? "For His sake I have accepted the loss of all things and I consider them so much rubbish, that I may gain Christ and be found in Him."[4] The Christ that Saint Paul encountered is no different from the Christ we have encountered. There is only one Christ, the real one, who was born, died, rose and is present today in the life of the Church, His mysterious Body, not the one of my thoughts or imagination, not the one of my interpretations. For Him, you can let everything else go because without Him all the rest has no value. All the rest is nothing compared to that "gain." Was Saint Paul crazy? Did John and Andrew follow Jesus because they were confused? Or were they more reasonable than everyone? It is a problem of the reasonableness of faith!

Each of us is called to decide whether it is worthwhile to risk for what you have encountered. Experience will provide the verification of your decision. And if you deem that Christ does not deserve your risk [and you leave], and then if tomorrow you realize that what you gained [looking elsewhere] is just crumbs, you can always return and seek those who have followed Christ

[3] Mt 13:44.
[4] Phil 3:8-9.

and by grace live a more desirable, dramatic and glad life. You will always be welcome. The heart of the problem is a judgement of esteem for what we have encountered, not just cheap sentimentalism! Sentimentalism does not move anything. What moves our "I" is a judgement of esteem for something that finally corresponds and that therefore we do not want to miss for anything in the world. If we have found it, it is our decision whether to follow or not. If we have not found it, the only thing to do is to await expectantly with our eyes wide open to glimpse some sign, as the poet Antonio Machado said, "on the shore of the great silence."[5]

"Yesterday you told us that Fr. Giussani said to you, 'in the end, the difference is between those who have done a stable work and those who have not.' Can you explain better what Fr. Giussani meant by 'a stable work'? What helps stability in this work?"

Fr. Giussani's goal in leaving the Venegono Seminary to teach religion in high school was to help young people perceive "the relevance of faith for the needs of life." When he walked up the three steps to the Berchet High school, this was his goal. He said it from the very beginning, "Because of my formation at home and in seminary, first, and my own reflections later, I was deeply convinced that, unless faith could be found

---

[5] A. Machado, "S'è addormentato il mio cuore? [Has my heart fallen asleep?]" LX, *Solitudini (1899-1907)*, in Id., *Tutte le poesie e prose scelte* [All Poems and Selected Prose] (Milan: Mondadori, 2010), 107. Our translation from the Italian translation.

and located in present experience, and confirmed by it, and useful for responding to its needs, it would not be able to endure in a world where everything, *everything*, said and says the opposite."[6]

Giussani was convinced this goal could be achieved only through a road, a method. What he proposed was fundamentally a method. He realized that a certain way of communicating the faith, the one received by the students he met at the Berchet High school and those he had previously heard in the confessional, was by then ineffective. Shortly after receiving the first initiation into the faith, those young people were no longer interested in Christianity. He understood that the problem was the way they were introduced to the faith, and that therefore the point was the adults. As our friend Lucio Brunelli wrote recently, "The crisis of the 'empty churches' comes from a long time ago, begins when the churches were full."[7] Giussani began teaching when churches were still full. He had understood where the problem stood: people no longer perceived faith as relevant for the needs of life, and so it was losing its interest. It was necessary to propose Christianity in its original nature as an event of

---

[6] L. Giussani, *The Risk of Education*, xxxii

[7] The article continues: "In the 1950s when Saint Peter's Square could not contain the overflowing crowd of green berets, a young Lombard priest decided to abandon his academic (and ecclesiastical) career to go teach religion in a public high school, the most secular one in Milan. During a train journey, speaking with some young people, that priest–his name was Luigi Giussani–realized just how much faith in Christ was a distant horizon in their life. Something was obstructing the almost natural mechanism by which the Christian tradition had been transmitted for centuries from parents to children." L. Brunelli, "Le chiese vuote e la fantasia di Dio [Empty churches and the imagination of God]," *L'Osservatore Romano*, p. 9. Our translation.

life; its reduction to discourse or ethics could not and cannot respond to human expectancy and attract the interest of real people. That is why I quoted Fr. Giussani's passage, "Human impact is what can jolt people today–an event that reechoes as initial event, when Jesus raised His eyes and said, 'Zacchaeus, come down here, I'm coming to your house'."

The encounter with the event makes the journey of a verification possible and necessary. As Giussani said, the Church cannot cheat, because "it is life, and it must offer life." Nor can the human person cheat, because "man's prospect is true journeying, but his heart must be willing."[8] This is what I called work. If we did not accept the journey presented to us in Giussani's proposal, we would not be able to endure. So what does this involve?

Life presents problems, and each of us faces them with the modality or hypothesis suggested by the context in which we live and that in some way we make ours. Thus in the field we verify its adequacy or inadequacy. This is what happened to me. In the 1970s I tried to face the problems of living related to my vocation and priestly task, starting from what I had received. Quite soon I realized that this modality that had been transmitted to me was not adequate. Deep down I remained ill at ease and uncomfortable. That was the period in which I met the Movement, in the late 1970s.

It was crucial for me to find myself in front of a man–Giussani–in whom I could see realized what I was unable to obtain with my original hypothesis. I

[8] L. Giussani, *Why the Church?*, 208.

did not have a sentimental reaction, because circumstances did not even allow me to see him often enough to have a close relationship. Instead, it was the clear recognition of a difference. Ever since then, I cannot even speak of things I experience without referring to that encounter. As I have said, the first times I went to the international gestures of the Movement, I only saw Giussani from a distance, like many of you, but the way he faced reality provoked a strong repercussion in me. I said to myself, "This is something different!" Since then, I have desired nothing other than to learn that way, to take on that gaze.

The key point that he insisted on was experience. Giussani constantly invited me to compare what happened in my life to the deep needs of my heart. This comparison is part of the method that characterized his proposal. "Since my first hour in the classroom I have always said: 'I am not here to make you adopt the ideas I will give you as your own, but to teach you a true method for judging the things I will say. And the things that I will say are an experience, which is the outcome of a long past: two thousand years'."[9] As I have said many times, in this way Giussani put in my hands the instrument for making a human journey. He used to say, Christ, the event of Christ, entrusts itself to the judgment of our experience.[10]

This reference to experience was crucial for me. Even when I made mistakes, I could always learn something. A friend recounted that she met a colleague, a researcher, in the hallway who was visibly

[9] L. Giussani, *The Risk of Education*, xxxi.
[10] Cfr. L. Giussani, *Why the Church?.*, 204-205.

sad. She asked why and the colleague said, "Because the experiment failed." So our friend replied, "But an experiment is always an experiment!" that is, it always teaches us something, and even when it fails, it is always a gain in the journey to get closer to the truth. So, in my experience every day, I perceived whether my way of facing things was adequate, whether my attempt responded to the need I had. Then when I found myself in front of Giussani, I compared how he faced things and how I faced them, and I saw what happened in him and what happened in me. I could not help but recognize an evident difference, a desirable newness.

If we look at the Gospel, this is what Jesus did with His disciples. They faced life according to the working hypothesis they had received as members of the people of Israel, until they encountered One in whom they perceived such a newness that they never left Him. From that time on they faced everything in His companionship. At the Easter Triduum of the university students I found myself thinking of Peter as I never had before. From the beginning, he got involved with Jesus. Giussani said, "From the first encounter, He filled his whole mind, his whole heart."[11] What was the risk that Peter ran, and that we run? Thinking that he already knew who the One standing in front of him was. "Who do the people say that the Son of Man is?" Jesus asked His disciples. "John the Baptist, others Elijah, still others Jeremiah or one of the prophets." "And you?" Peter was the first to

[11] L. Giussani-S. Alberto-J. Prades, *Generating Traces in the History of the World*, 60.

answer. "You are the Messiah, the Son of the living God." "Good, Peter! Because you did not come up with this answer, but the Father revealed it to you." A moment later, "Jesus began to show His disciples that He must go to Jerusalem and suffer greatly from the elders, the chief priests, and the scribes, and be killed and on the third day be raised." Peter, who thought he already understood everything and knew who Jesus was, said, "God forbid, Lord! No such thing shall ever happen to you." And Jesus said, "Get behind me, Satan! You are an obstacle to me. You are thinking not as God does, but as human beings do."[12]

Peter's whole life was marked by the continual comparison between his way of being in reality and that of Christ, between his measure and that of Christ. This stable work of comparison was the key thing for Peter, precisely because of the correspondence he had experienced in the encounter with Jesus, and that motivated Peter to follow Him. He did not understand what Jesus proposed each time and in each moment. For example, the fact that Jesus had to go to Jerusalem to die did not fit with Peter's expectations. "No, no, it's impossible!" But think of the washing of the disciples' feet. Let's imagine Peter, who had a boundless passion for Jesus, when he saw Him get up from the table and get ready to wash the disciples' feet. Peter clashed again with His profound difference. For Peter, this gesture was too much. "No! You wash *my* feet?" Jesus answered, "Peter, now you do not understand what I'm doing, but later you will." At that point, the question was whether it was reasonable to follow Him even

[12] Cf. Mt 16,13-23.

if he did not understand. Impetuously, Peter said, "No way!" But as in other occasions, in crucial situations, Jesus did not compromise with anyone, much less Peter, and insisted, "If I do not wash your feet, you will have no part of Me!" Peter gave in; he could no longer oppose Him. "If You put it that way, then not only my feet, but my hands and head as well."[13] Why did he accept? Because having lived with Jesus for three years and having ceaselessly compared what that man said and did with the needs of his heart, he could not fail to recognize even when he did not or could not yet understand, that only He had the words of eternal life. "If we leave You, where will we go?" His attachment to that man, full of reasons, was stronger than all his lack of understanding, all his littleness.

The stable work suggested by Giussani does not require a Harvard degree. It is for everyone, for people like Peter, like you and me. It is not a problem of particular "intelligence," not a bookish question, not a complication, but a constant comparison between a presence and your own heart, between a presence and your own attempt to face daily challenges, between His measure and yours. What was more interesting for Peter than this constant comparison between his attempt and what he saw Jesus do? If Jesus had not been irreducible to Peter's interpretations, or if Peter had left every time things did not dovetail with his image, he would have lost the best part. The fundamental problem of the method is all here. In a certain context, Giussani said that "the grave problem of the Movement, the very grave problem of the leaders, is

[13] Cf. Jn 13:6-9.

that they speak the discourse [...] but they do not have the method." He added, "The translation of ideas into method demands something that [...] I fear not even those who have done the first volume of the School of Community have[14] [a thing that] enters into the conception, the structure of reason [...]: affection. [...] This introduces the most important aspect of the method: without affection you do not know. [...] Knowledge is open eyes. Reality is empty if it does not strike you. The repercussion of reality on your eyes is called affection, *affectus*. [...] Therefore, the method is tied to the word affection. Affection concludes the recognition of reality, or in other words the recognition of the Movement, inasmuch as it makes explicit the modality with which the Movement corresponds to and actuates [pay attention here!] the fundamental needs that define the human heart. The heart is not the wellspring of sentiment, it is the wellspring of complete reason." Having said this, Giussani wondered, "Why is there this resistance to the method?" Why do people resist, after they have perceived Christ to be so corresponding to their heart? Why did Peter resist? Because "freedom is like a dagger that enters between knowledge and the *affectus* and tries to remove *affectus* from itself, exalting pure knowledge (rationalism) or exalting pure affection (instinctivism, empiricism)."[15]

---

[14] The reference is to L. Giussani, *The Religious Sense*.

[15] "President's Council." October 11, 1994," typewritten document conserved in the General Secretariat of CL, Milan. See also L. Giussani, *L'autocoscienza del cosmo* [The Self-Awareness of the Cosmos] (Milan: Bur, 2000), 278-279. Our translation.

In order to follow the method, it is necessary to follow a law, and if this law is not respected, freedom errs. "In order to affirm yourself, you need to affirm an Other."[16] Having encountered one in whom we have seen the fullest realization of our "I" (as said in some of the testimonies I quoted), we understand how affirming another is not the renunciation of reason but the full affirmation of it, because affirming this other is the affirmation of yourself. But if you do not do this "stable work," if you do not constantly compare yourself and the presence encountered, you cannot understand. What would have been of Peter if he had not affirmed Christ? What would have been of us if we had not followed Giussani?

"There is only one thing you have to learn from me: how to learn,"[17] Giussani said in 1978. Are we willing to learn, to do a stable work? I can verify in my experience what I manage to obtain by following my own measure instead of following the presence I recognized as corresponding to the expectancy of my heart. If I do not go beyond my measure, I do not grow, I do not acquire the human stature that made Peter a protagonist, the beginning of a new people. Jesus was entirely concerned with generating Peter, because without Peter nothing would have remained, nothing, nothing! The genius of Giussani was to have linked Peter's *yes* to the generation of a people. It is possible

---

[16] "President's Council." October 11, 1994," typewritten document conserved in the General Secretariat of CL, Milan. Our translation.

[17] L. Giussani quoted in A. Savorana, *Life of Luigi Giussani* (Montreal: McGill-Queen's University Press, 2018), 567.

to become a protagonist like Peter. We just have to allow ourselves to be generated by Him.

"I'd like you to explain better your answer to the girl who said, 'I see that the love I experience comes from my mother and father, my friends, and I don't understand well how at a certain point Christ comes into play. Is the affection of my family members, the good of children and grandchildren, the manifestation of Christ or not? Even non-Christians love each other. For me, often, Christ is a stamp glued on, but it doesn't stick."

"Can Christ become familiar only through witnesses? In this way, isn't there the risk of limiting the possibility of the event? What is the value of the sacraments, the liturgy, revelation through the Holy Scriptures, and personal prayer for reaching certainty in faith?"

When a young man asked me the first question, I answered, "When you go to bed in the evening, can you say with certainty that your mother loves you? It is not a matter of intense reasoning. Can you explain all the things she has done for you as anything other than signs of her love? Or do you think they are motivated by self-interest (for example, wanting you to take care of her in her old age)? Tell me whether any other interpretations of the signs, other than her love for you, are convincing. The signs you see point to a meaning you do not see, your mother's love. What you are dealing with are signs." I added, "The same thing happens with the Christian event. The signs are different and cannot be compared to those of a mother, but the dynamic is the same. Tell me if you can reduce the humanity you see testified in certain people to the fact that they are good, nice, polite, generous–finish the list with the possible interpretations–or whether instead it points to something you cannot see and cannot define, but is involved in what you see."

This is the point. The recognition that there is another factor in this companionship we have come upon. I cannot define it, but it exists. The recognition that certain human results that I see, certain human resonances that are documented in it, point to something I cannot see, but I cannot help but admit is there. If I eliminated it, I would not be able to explain the experience I have. In this companionship, in the people I have encountered–within, not outside, within!–there is something irreducible. The way certain people live, facing life and death, has no other explanation but the reference to something mysterious that I do not see. If I suppress it, I erase the origin of that difference. In the first example, I erase the love of which I see the signs, and at the same time make the signs senseless. I cannot detect love with a machine; there is no algorithm that can calculate it, but this does not mean it does not exist. Imagine a young woman who has children. How can she show them her love, if not through signs? How could Jesus show His disciples who He was, if not through signs? How can we reach certainty in faith, if not through the signs of His presence, now, in the present and not just as memories of the past?

Moving quickly to the second question, without something present, the liturgy would not speak to us. We see it in the Gospel: when Jesus is present, His disciples understand the words of the Bible and everything the prophets had said. Christ opened their gaze to the understanding of the Scriptures and the prophecies. Yes, the liturgy is the source, but at the same time our heart needs to be constantly thrown wide open to it so that when we hear that Christ is risen, we will not remain indifferent, as Brunelli said in the article I quoted, and as happens to many people today. The ultimate, mysterious origin of our faith is the event we celebrate in the liturgy and that constantly challenges our reason and freedom. In fact, it is in our heart that everything that happens must find space.

"You have shown us how in dramatic situations like death, suffering, and evil, uncertainty challenges hope. But in the routine things that happen to us every day, how can we keep hope alive? How should we act when we are not slapped by an extreme and dramatic situation?"

"It is so easy to be entangled in our remorse and the mistakes we have made, to the point of not being able to see His eyes, not recognizing His presence! Certainly, this is the experience that most challenges my hope."

The answer to the first question is very easy. Either a heart attack or education, as I often say with a paradoxical image. The one alternative to waiting for dramatic circumstances to waken us, is participation in a place that cannot be reduced to ourselves, that educates us to keep hope alive. This is what Jesus did with His disciples. He did not introduce them to hope primarily through dramatic circumstances, but with the attraction of His presence. Analagously, Giussani did not introduce us to reality and hope through a dramatic circumstance, but through an irreducible attraction that moved us deeply, something that dramatic circumstances cannot obtain. Ultimately, there is no alternative to continual education, because even when we get past certain dramatic situations we easily return to the same old same old. This is the risk we run with the pandemic: we can close this dramatic vicissitude as if nothing had happened. If our life is not immersed in a place that continually regenerates us by challenging us, it becomes almost impossible not to yield to the nothingness of a life without meaning, suffocating in our daily routine.

The same can be said of remorse. In front of One who says to you and to me, as He did to Peter after being denied three times, "Do you love Me?"[18] the problem is certainly not remorse for our idiocies. Peter denied Him; he made the biggest mistake a person can make, in huge letters and in front of everyone (something else altogether from remorse for our own big or little errors!). Here you see the heart of the problem. Peter documented it even before his *yes* to Christ. The disciples went out to fish and had caught nothing. From the shore came a cry, "Why don't you cast the net over the right side of the boat?" The nets came up overfilled and groaning from the weight! John–acute–exclaimed: "It's the Lord!" and Peter immediately jumped in the water to swim to shore.[19] Peter's affection for Christ was more powerful than his remorse.

[18] Cf. Jn 21:15.
[19] Cf. Jn 21:1-7.

Jesus had not yet asked him, "Do you love Me?" but Peter's affection was so rooted in his innermost being that not even his triple denial could remove it. This is the only thing that vanquishes remorse: the prevalence of a Presence and affection greater than itself. As Giussani said, speaking of Peter's *yes*: you need a presence to whom you can say *yes*.

Such great affection for Christ grows in us that no matter what mistake we have made or might make, we will never be separated from Him.

TABLE OF CONTENTS